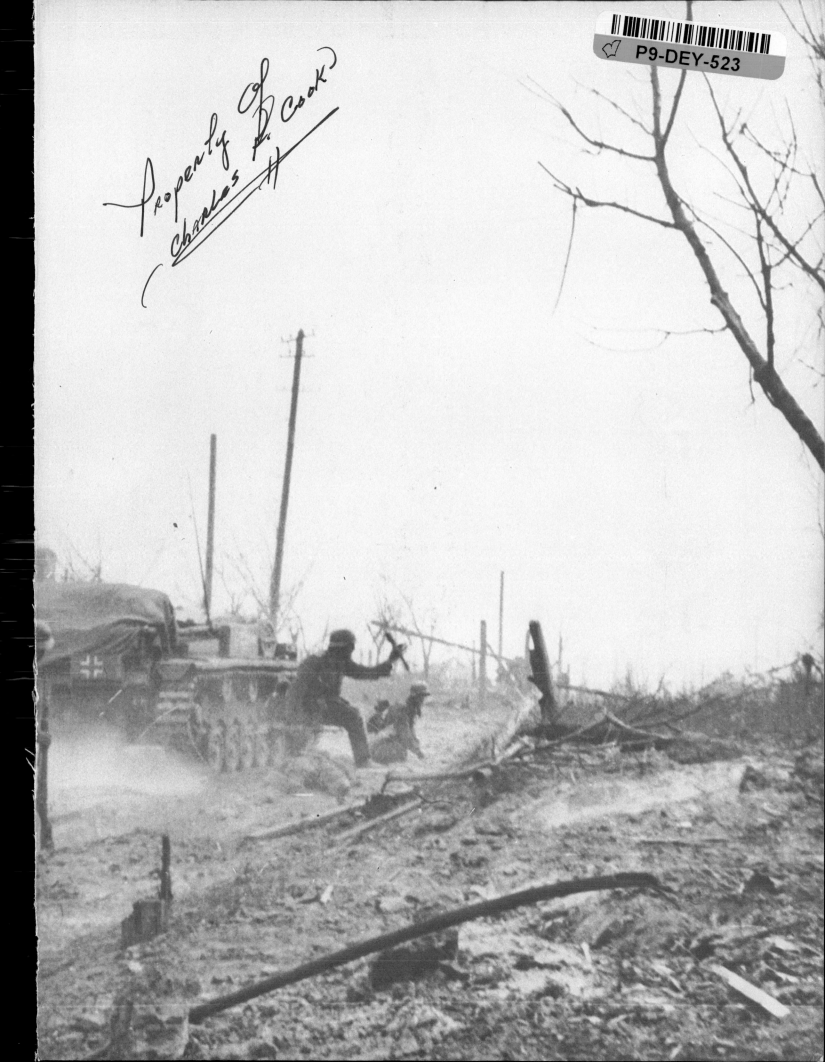

WORLD WAR II
IN PHOTOGRAPHS

WORLD WAR II
IN PHOTOGRAPHS
JOHN PIMLOTT

The Military Press
New York

Editor Adrian Gilbert
Designer Michael Hodson
Picture editor Robert Hunt

Photograph, previous page: Under fire, Free French Foreign
Legionnaires rush from their positions during the battle of
Gazala, June 1942. *Photograph, half-title:* Soviet infantry launch
an attack against a German strongpoint on the Eastern Front.
Photograph, endpapers: Alongside a StuG III assault gun
a German infantry section goes into battle during the
fighting for Stalingrad, late in 1942.

Picture acknowledgments: Archiv Ustavu Marxismu-
Leninismu, Australian War Memorial, Bundesarchiv, Camera
Press, Crown Copyright, CTK Prague, Carina Dvorak, ECPA,
Robert Hunt Library, Imperial War Museum, Keystone,
Ministry of Information, National Archives, Novosti, Bruce
Robertson, Service International Photographique, Ullstein,
UPI, US Air Force, US Army, US Coast Guard, US Information
Agency, US Marine Corps, US Navy, Wojskowa Agencja
Fotograficzna.

© 1984 by Orbis Publishing, London
First published in Great Britain by
Orbis Publishing Limited, London

This 1985 edition published by
The Military Press, distributed
by Crown Publishers, Inc.

Printed in Great Britain by
BAS Printers Limited, Over Wallop, Hampshire

Library of Congress Cataloging in Publication Data

Pimlott, John.
   World War II In Photographs.

   Bibliography: p.
   Includes index.
   1. World War, 1939–1945––Campaigns.   I. Title.
D743.P525   1984   940.54'1'0222   84.16623
ISBN 0-517-44290-6

h   g   f   e   d   c   b   a

Contents

Introduction   6

The rise of Hitler   8

The German triumphs 1939–40   10

North Africa and the Balkans 1940–42   28

From Barbarossa to Stalingrad   42

Pearl Harbor and after   56

Victory in North Africa   70

The Battle of the Atlantic   82

The Russian steamroller   94

Battle for the Pacific   108

The Italian campaign   120

Invasion of Europe   132

The bomber offensive on Germany   150

The end in Europe   164

The fall of Japan   176

Index and bibliography   190

Introduction

World War II was a 'total war'. Although it began in September 1939 as an essentially regional conflict between Germany and the Anglo-French allies over the future of Poland, it rapidly developed into an ideological contest, with each side – Axis and Allies – intent upon the complete destruction of its rival. It culminated in the use of atomic bombs against Japan in August 1945, by which time over 50 million people had died and the shape of world politics had been radically altered. World War II contributed to the decline of Europe, accelerated the development of the United States and Soviet Union as superpowers and triggered the process of European decolonisation. These are legacies with which we continue to live.

The war had its origins in the terms of the Versailles peace treaty, signed in June 1919 to mark the end of the 'Great War' of 1914–18. The treaty represented an attempt by the victors of that war – Britain, France, Italy and the United States – to prevent a repetition of the recent catastrophe, and the problem was tackled in three ways. Firstly, the states-structure of central Europe was completely reshaped. The Austro-Hungarian Empire (where the war had been sparked off and which

had, in any case, collapsed by 1918) was dismembered; Austria became a small, weak state, Hungary was reduced in size, and new nations – Czechoslovakia and Yugoslavia – were created. Germany was reduced territorially, losing land to Czechoslovakia and the reborn state of Poland. Secondly, Germany – the arch-enemy of 1914–18 – was weakened economically, politically and militarily. France regained Alsace-Lorraine (lost in the Franco-Prussian War of 1870–71) and occupied the Saar industrial area; huge reparations for war damage were exacted by the victors; Germany's overseas empire was dismembered and the size of her armed forces cut to 100,000 men, with tanks, aircraft and submarines prohibited. In addition, the Rhineland was demilitarised and key areas of Germany occupied by Allied troops, the latter to last until the reparations (set at 132 billion gold marks) had been paid. Thirdly, an international body, the League of Nations, was created, within which minor crises could be defused through discussion or collective action before they developed into major wars.

Unfortunately these measures produced more problems than they solved. The problem of com-

2 German troops – members of the 'Condor Legion' – watch as Nationalist forces under General Francisco Franco conduct the final campaign of the Spanish Civil War around Toledo, March 1939. German aid to Franco proved useful in testing new weapons and tactical doctrines.

3 German motor-cycle troops enter Prague, 15 March 1939. Despite the Munich Agreement of September 1938, Hitler did not curtail his territorial demands: his takeover of what was left of Czechoslovakia in March 1939, however, signalled the end of Anglo-French appeasement.

peting nationalisms in central Europe was not solved at Versailles: substantial German minorities in Poland and Czechoslovakia gave German nationalists a theme to trumpet, and the latent antagonisms between all the new states – between Hungary and Czechoslovakia for example – produced a potential for conflict. As neither the United States nor the Soviet Union joined the League of Nations, the role of world policeman was left in the hands of Britain and France, both of whom were weak after four years of war. More importantly, Versailles humiliated the Germans, causing deep resentment and a desire for revenge, and left the country too weak to meet the reparations demands. In 1923 there was a massive inflation and the German currency collapsed. France rubbed salt in the wounds by occupying the Ruhr as security against the outstanding debt, and although the Dawes Plan (1924) introduced a revised payment scheme which eased the financial burden, irreparable economic damage had been done. Massive inflation and high unemployment opened the door to political extremists.

The most active of these extremists were the National Socialists (Nazis) under the leadership of Adolf Hitler, whose charismatic oratory and promises of recovery gathered a steady momentum of support. In January 1933, after substantial Nazi gains in democratic elections to the *Reichstag* (parliament), he was appointed Chancellor. He immediately set about consolidating his power base, discrediting his main rivals – the communists – by implicating them in the *Reichstag* fire of February 1933 and strengthening his hold on the country by means of the Nazi Party machine, backed by the thugs of the SA (*Sturmabteilungen*) and their successors the SS (*Schutzstaffel*). By August 1934 Hitler was strong enough to declare himself *Führer* ('leader') of a German state which no longer enjoyed the benefits of democracy. Amid new laws to suppress trades unions, opposition parties, Jews and other 'non-Aryans', a totalitarian dictatorship emerged.

Hitler was also active on the international scene, aiming to recover lost territories and reassert the German voice in world politics. Although an attempt to seize power in Austria in July 1934 was thwarted, his long-term intentions were indicated as he blatantly overturned the Versailles treaty and began to rearm, concentrating upon aggressive instruments of war such as tanks and bomber aircraft. The League was powerless to intervene, having already been seen to fail in 1931 when Japan invaded Manchuria and this was followed by a lack of effective response to an Italian seizure of Abyssinia (Ethiopia) four years later. The way was clear for Hitler to initiate more aggressive moves.

These began in March 1936, when German troops reoccupied the Rhineland without being opposed by Britain or France. Thus emboldened, Hitler offered open support to General Franco's Nationalists in the Spanish Civil War (1936–39), using the conflict as a testing ground for the new weapons and tactical doctrines of Germany's armed forces. Indeed, as the Luftwaffe showed its new capabilities by bombing Spanish towns, the states of the West began to express deep fears for the safety of their own populations and adopted deliberate policies of appeasement as Hitler continued to demand *lebensraum* ('living space') for the German people. Britain and France did nothing to oppose a Nazi takeover of Austria in March 1938 and even went so far as to sanction the dismemberment of Czechoslovakia six months later at Munich, in response to Hitler's call for a return of the Sudetenland to Germany.

But there were limits beyond which France and Britain and their allies refused to go. A German invasion of the remains of Czechoslovakia in March 1939 forced them to prepare for the inevitability of war and when Hitler made his next demand – for the return of the Danzig Corridor from Poland – appeasement gave way to a firmer political resolve. Thus, when German troops invaded Poland on 1 September 1939 the Western Allies delivered an ultimatum for their withdrawal. When this ran out at 1100 hours on the 3rd, Great Britain declared war, followed by France a short while later.

The Rise of Hitler

1927.

1 The Nazi leadership, Nuremberg, August 1927. From left to right: Heinrich Himmler, future head of the SS; Rudolf Hess, Hitler's secretary and future deputy; Gregor Strasser (looking over Hitler's right shoulder), influential leader of the affiliated *Völkisch* movement; Adolf Hitler, leader of the NSDAP and future ruler of Germany; Captain Franz Pfeffer von Salomon, then head of the SA.

2 The indoctrination of youth: German girls, following the example of their teachers, give the Nazi salute as storm troopers march past. The infiltration and eventual control of education in Germany was a key factor in the expansion and maintenance of Nazi power.

4

3 Leader of the SS and one of the most powerful men in the Nazi hierarchy, Heinrich Himmler considers a close-cropped inmate of the first Nazi concentration camp at Dachau near Munich, May 1936.

4 The face of Nazi oppression: SA and SS troopers plaster a clothes shop with posters warning shoppers not to buy from Jews, Berlin 1933. Anti-semitism was a central feature of Nazi policy and from as early as 1933 Jews were excluded from the civil service, law, journalism and entertainment. It was the beginning of a process which was to lead to the death of nearly six million European Jews by 1945.

5 The power of the Nazi Party: storm troopers march through the streets of Nuremberg in a bombastic display of strength.

Chapter 1
The German triumphs 1939-40

1 Allied commanders pose for the camera during the Battle of France, May 1940. From left to right: General Sir William Ironside, Chief of the Imperial Staff; Winston Churchill, newly-appointed prime minister of Britain; General Maurice Gamelin, C-in-C of the French Army; General Viscount Gort VC, C-in-C of the BEF; General Alphonse Georges, commander of the Northeast Front.

2 Winston Spencer Churchill, prime minister of Britain from May 1940 until virtually the end of the war. He came to epitomise the dogged determination of the country to resist the fascist threat, sustaining domestic morale through a series of stirring radio broadcasts.

3 Field Marshal Fedor von Bock, one of the most distinguished of Germany's generals in the early war years. He commanded army groups during the campaigns in Poland (1939), the Low Countries (1940) and Russia (1941), before being relieved for 'health reasons' in December (1941). He was killed in an air raid in 1945.

4 The 'Panzer corridor': the German advance on the Channel.

The German invasion of Poland in September 1939 was the beginning of a swift and ruthless campaign. Army Group North (Field-Marshal von Bock) attacked from Pomerania and East Prussia, aiming to link up at Lodz, Warsaw and Brest Litovsk with elements of Army Group South (Field-Marshal von Runstedt), advancing out of Silesia, in a series of wide enveloping moves. The plan worked well: Poland's air force was destroyed in the first two days, leaving poorly equipped and badly deployed ground units to be split up and encircled by fast-moving armour. An extemporised counter-attack, during which horsed cavalry was vainly pitted against the Panzers, enjoyed some success on the Bzura River, west of Warsaw (9–15 September), but on the 17th a Russian invasion from the east sealed the country's fate. Warsaw, devastated by air and artillery bombardment, fell to the Germans on 27 September, whereupon Poland – the first victim of Blitzkrieg ('lightning war') – was divided between the victors. The campaign had taken just 18 days.

The speed of German victory helped persuade the British and French to remain behind the fixed defences of the Maginot Line along the Franco-German border, and as the Wehrmacht slowly redeployed from the east, little fighting took place on the Western Front. There were, however, major engagements elsewhere: on 30 November 1939 Russia invaded Finland, crossing the border at a number of points from Petsamo in the north to Karelia in the south. At first the campaign was a disaster – a combination of weather, terrain and stubborn Finnish resistance caused enormous Russian casualties – but after a period of reorganisation and reinforcement a major new offensive forced the Finns to sign away significant tracts of territory on 12 March 1940.

In itself this 'Winter War' was peripheral to the developing world war, but Britain and France did prepare forces to go to Finland's aid in early 1940.

They were still available on 9 April when Germany suddenly attacked Denmark and Norway. The Danes sued for peace within 24 hours, but as the Norwegians retained defensive viability despite air and naval landings at Narvik, Trondheim, Bergen, Stavanger, Kristiansand and Oslo, the Anglo-French expeditionary force was hurriedly committed. As it moved towards Trondheim and Narvik, the Royal Navy secured a remarkable degree of sea supremacy, sinking 10 German destroyers in the two 'Battles of Narvik' (10 and 13 April), and this enabled landings to be made on the 14th. But the Allied troops lacked adequate air cover and were ill-suited to the Norwegian terrain: on 1 May Trondheim was evacuated, and although Narvik was wrested from German hands on the 28th, it too was abandoned on 8 June. Norway came under full German control.

Withdrawal from Narvik had been hastened by the emergence of a greater threat, for on 10 May German forces invaded France and the Low Countries. It was a brilliant campaign. Key locations, including the fortress of Eben Emael, were seized by airborne troops, paving the way for an infantry-orientated assault on Holland and Belgium by von Bock's Army Group B. To the British and French this was reminiscent of 1914 and they pushed the bulk of their mobile forces into Belgium to oppose the advance. As they did so, however, armoured divisions from von Runstedt's Army Group A advanced westwards through the 'impassable' Ardennes, crossed the Meuse River on 14 May and motored towards the Channel coast, spreading panic among rear-area units and threatening to drive a wedge between the Allies in Belgium and their bases in northern France. By then the Dutch had surrendered (14 May) and the Allied air forces had been virtually destroyed; despite a British counter-attack from Arras on 21 May, the Panzers reached the coast at Noyelles and struck north towards Boulogne and Calais as the British and French forces caught in Belgium withdrew to Dunkirk. The Belgians surrendered on 28 May.

By then the British had begun to evacuate their troops from Dunkirk, an operation (code-named 'Dynamo') that was to continue under air and artillery attack until 4 June, saving 338,226 men but leaving behind 2472 guns, 63,879 vehicles and 500,000 tons of supplies. The Germans, joined on 10 June by the Italians, proceeded to concentrate against the remaining French forces, occupying Paris on 14 June and advancing south as far as the Spanish border. Marshal Pétain, the new French premier, had no choice but to accept a humiliating armistice, signed on the 22nd, which split his

country into two zones – that in the north occupied **2**
by the Germans and that in the south administered
by a collaborationist government based in Vichy.

Hitler immediately ordered a seaborne invasion
of Britain (Operation 'Sealion') to be prepared, and
as barges were gathered in the Channel ports the
Luftwaffe was given the task of gaining air supremacy. On 10 July German aircraft attacked
convoys in the Channel but the RAF, mindful that its
600 front-line fighters were outnumbered by an
enemy force of over 3000 fighters and bombers,
refused to rise to the bait. Only when the Luftwaffe
changed its tactics on 12 August and attacked
airfields in southern England was the RAF committed to the battle in earnest and for over a month
radar-assisted Spitfires and Hurricanes of Fighter
Command fought for control of the skies, slowly
gaining the upper hand. By early September the
Luftwaffe had been forced to change tactics yet
again, this time in favour of bombing raids on
London, and on 15 September, in a series of
running dogfights which left 60 German aircraft
destroyed, the 'Battle of Britain' reached a climax.
Although substantial damage was to be inflicted on
British cities in a 'Blitz' that was to last until May
1941, Sealion was cancelled on 12 October 1940,
and Britain was safe from invasion. Her position
was, however, perilous in the extreme, with most of
western Europe under German control, with Italy
threatening her possessions in the Middle East,
and with her continued survival dependent upon
the fragile life-line of seaborne supplies.

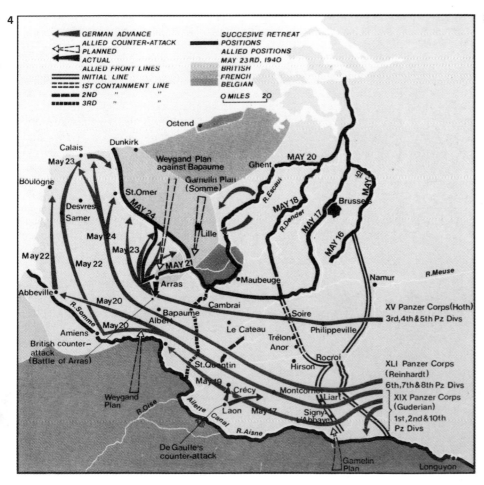

Poland 1939

1 Polish lancers prepare to oppose the German advance across the Bzura River on 9 September 1939. Their valour was no substitute for modern weapons, and they stood no chance against German armour.

2 The destruction of the Polish Air Force in the first few days of the war gave the Luftwaffe freedom of the skies. Here a Heinkel He-111 unloads its bombs onto an undefended Polish city.

3 SS troops – members of a reinforced infantry battalion drawn from local SS, police and Nazi Party personnel and known as SS *Heimwehr* (Home Guard) *Danzig* – move cautiously towards the Post Office in Danzig, September 1939. The attack against Danzig was the prelude to the German Army's invasion of Poland.

4 A disadvantage of Blitzkrieg: as the armour raced ahead, many of its support units, still dependent upon the horse for mobility, struggled to keep up.

5 The face of defeat: Polish soldiers captured near Warsaw march off under German guard; many of them were never to see Poland again.

6 The end in Poland: German horse-drawn artillery enters Warsaw, 27 September 1939, through a city showing clear evidence of the air and artillery bombardment that preceded the surrender. Warsaw was only the first of Europe's great cities that were to experience the horrors of mass air attack.

Phoney War
The Western Front 1939-40

1 French and British troops prepare to toast in the New Year, 1 January 1940. Their light-hearted optimism was to be brutally dashed in the coming months. Although the quality of the British Expeditionary Force was generally of a high standard, the fighting abilities of many French formations remained suspect

2 Inside the Maginot Line: French soldiers maintain the huge generators needed to provide heat, light and power inside the fortifications.

3 French troops man a machine-gun position in the Maginot Line. Their confidence in the impregnable nature of the defences contributed to a lack of Allied flexibility, tying units to static positions which, in the event, could be by-passed. The Maginot line was started in 1929 and reflected the French Army's belief in the strength of the defensive. Hoping to avoid a repetition of the costly battles of Word War I, French military planners failed to take into account the possibilities for offensive warfare offered by the armoured vehicle and the aeroplane.

4 March 1940: with many men away in the French Army, farms were short of labour, and as a gesture of goodwill, British troops (such as these members of the Royal Artillery) were often drafted in to help.

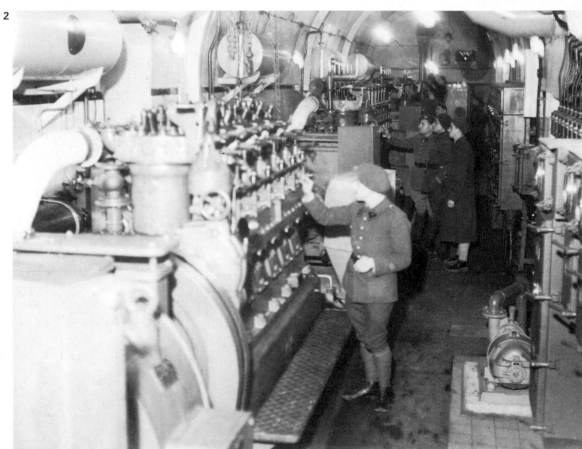

5 Soldiers of the Welsh Guards fraternise with Polish troops in the French Army on the Western Front; a photograph taken in early May 1940, only hours before the German attack.

6 British troops in the snow of January 1940. Their dugout is reminiscent of the Western Front in World War I and was indicative of a backward-looking defensive mentality that was soon to be destroyed by the technology of armoured Blitzkrieg.

7 Two Vickers water-cooled machine guns, manned by soldiers of the Manchester Regiment, stand guard in front of a French headquarters in March 1940. The close Allied co-operation implied by this photograph did not exist in practice.

Fall of Norway

1 German infantry advance into the mountains of Norway. According to the original caption, the group was under Norwegian sniper fire when the photograph was taken. The German soldier was generally well equipped and the men in this picture are armed with the standard infantry rifle of the German Army, the 7·92mm 98K, as well as the highly effective MG34 machine gun.

2 French *chasseurs alpins* prepare to embark for Norway, 10 April 1940. They had been earmarked originally for commitment to Finland, but the Russo-Finnish armistice of March 1940 left them free for other service. The *chasseurs alpins* were elite troops and their mountain warfare skills were highly valued during the fighting in Norway.

3 Armed with a 7·5mm M24/29 Chatellerault light machine gun, French troops man a position overlooking a fjord in southern Norway.

4 German infantry advance through a burning Norwegian village. Despite the dramatic nature of this photograph, the level of destruction in Norway was slight compared to the later campaigns in France and Russia.

5 Sheltering behind PzKpfw I light tanks German troops advance against Norwegian positions. The PzKpfw I was armed with just two MG34 machine guns and its lack of effective armour ensured that it was only used in support roles. It was withdrawn when more effective marks entered service.

6 Narvik harbour in the aftermath of the naval engagements of 10 and 13 April 1940. The wrecked and burning shipping shows the impact of the Royal Navy and the restricted area in which the battles took place.

Breakthrough in the West
The German offensive against France

1 The symbol of Blitzkrieg:
a Junkers Ju-87B Stuka
dive-bomber, sirens
howling, drops a full bomb-
load onto a ground target.
Air superiority was essential
before such machines could
be employed but once
committed their impact was
often considerable, helping
to undermine the morale of
the enemy and preparing the
way for the armour to
advance.

2 German paratroopers
jump from a Junkers
Ju-52/3 transport aircraft
over Holland, May 1940.
This operation was the first
in which such troops had
been used; the element of
surprise was to contribute to
Allied demoralisation and
defeat.

3 Paratroopers rush to
regroup on their drop-zone
in Holland, May 1940. The
machine gun is a tripod-
mounted MG34.

4 A German PzKpfw III advances across a field in Belgium on the second day of the great German offensive into the Low Countries. In 1940, the PzKpfw III was armed with a 3·7cm anti-tank gun and was employed in conjunction with the PzKpfw IV (7·5cm low-velocity gun) as the cutting edge of Germany's Panzer divisions.

5 A Luftwaffe-manned 8·8cm anti-aircraft gun, which, when used in a direct-fire, anti-tank role, posed a major problem for Allied armour. The gun shown here seems to be occupying a rather exposed position, but the innovative nature of its ground role and the lack of any air threat is probably sufficient protection.

6 The advance into Belgium in May 1940: An SdKfz 7 half-track artillery tractor tows an 8·8cm anti-aircraft gun past motor-cycle troops. The mobility of German artillery was an important factor in the success of the mechanised formations which were driving a fatal wedge between the Allied armies.

France defeated

1 French Renault R-35 light tanks advance under fire in 1940. Allied armour was rarely used in this way, being dissipated in 'penny-packets' in support of infantry. The R-35 was well-armoured by 1940 standards but its maximum road speed of only 20km/h (12mph) was a serious disadvantage for a light tank.

2 Remarkably cheerful (the original caption says 'drunk') French tank troops surrender to advancing German units, May 1940. Demoralised by the speed and power of the German assault, bewildered French soldiers had no choice but to give in.

3 A French howitzer gun-crew prepare their weapon for firing. Once the German attack materialised, few gunners were able to prepare positions like this, being forced to abandon their equipment in the confusion of retreat.

4 Amidst the roar of battle, French troops, clinging to the back of a tank, move through a burning town.

5 The surrender: French and German representatives sign the documents on 22 June 1940. On Hitler's insistence the ceremony took place in the same railway carriage at Compiègne that had been used for the German surrender in 1918.

6 Honour in defeat: German troops, impressed by the conduct of the French defenders of Lille, allow the garrison to march out to surrender with bayonets fixed, June 1940. The defence of Lille by the French First Army was important in gaining time for the Allied evacuation from Dunkirk.

7 A German horse-drawn unit marches through Paris to ram home the humiliation of France. Many such units were merely 'staging through', on their way to take part in the advance towards the Spanish border.

Dunkirk
Disaster and triumph

1 British 3·7in anti-aircraft guns, barrels split to render them useless to the enemy, lie abandoned outside Dunkirk, symbols of the heavy equipment losses of a disastrous campaign.

2 British and French survivors of a ship destroyed at Dunkirk are picked up by another vessel. They are fortunate – many such survivors had to return to the beaches and wait, often in vain, for another chance.

3 A column of French prisoners marches away from Dunkirk, with the oil-storage tanks ablaze in the background. Vichy propaganda was later to make much of the fact that Dunkirk was a predominantly British rescue operation, suggesting that French troops had been deliberately prevented from boarding rescue ships. There is little to substantiate this claim, especially as out of a total of 338,226 Allied troops evacuated some 113,000 were French.

4 A German soldier, equipped for battle, poses beside abandoned British artillery tractors outside Dunkirk. He is holding a Bergmann MP34 sub-machine gun and has a Luger pistol stuffed into his boot.

5 The enduring symbol of Dunkirk: British troops form orderly lines snaking down to the water's edge and the waiting boats. The photograph shows how vulnerable to air attack the troops were and how important were the largely unseen efforts of the RAF in protecting them.

6 A dejected column of British and French walking wounded winds its way off the Dunkirk beaches into captivity. The building in the background was used during the evacuation as a casualty clearing station.

Battle of Britain
RAF versus Luftwaffe

1 Inside the sector operations centre at Duxford during the battle. The centralised control of available fighter aircraft was a major factor in British success, preventing a dissipation of resources and ensuring that, whenever a threat was seen to emerge through the coastal radar sets, a reaction could be organised.

2 A line-up of Hawker Hurricane Mark I fighters, No 87 Squadron, August 1939. The pilots are rushing to board their aircraft as part of an exercise; many of them would be repeating the process for real within the year.

3 A Supermarine Spitfire Mark I. Of the aircraft available in 1940, the Spitfire was the most memorable, combining grace, manoeuvrability and hitting power.

4 Hurricane Is in line astern. Despite being overshadowed in the public mind by the Spitfire, there were more Hurricanes than Spitfires involved in the Battle of Britain. Together, the two types made a winning combination.

5 A group of Heinkel He-111 bombers flies towards southern England on a daylight raid, August 1940. It was the need to protect these aircraft that tied down the German fighters, denying them a freedom of action which could have caused problems to the RAF.

6 A German pilot, complete with Iron Cross First Class and Pilot's Qualification Badge, enjoys a drink and a cigarette provided by his police and army captors. German aircrew losses were severe, particularly as many survivors were forced to bale out over England, and were automatically taken prisoner.

7 Luftwaffe pilots, their Messerschmitt Bf-109E fighters in the background, relax between operations at a forward airstrip in France, summer 1940. Similar scenes on British airfields are an enduring image.

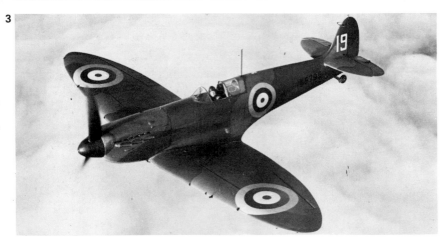

Blitz on Britain

1 St Paul's Cathedral, outlined in the smoke of a bombing raid, seemed to epitomise the survival of Britain during the Blitz.

2 A Heinkel He-111 flies over London during the daylight raid of 7 September 1940. The clear view of the target shows the advantage of day bombing, presuming that enemy defences are not active. The losses inflicted by the RAF on the day bombers forced the Luftwaffe to switch to night operations, with all their attendant problems of target location.

3 London ablaze: Tower Bridge against a backcloth of fires, started during the raids of early September. If these had been allowed to continue, London would have suffered significant economic damage.

4 A consequence of the bombing. Families, bombed out of their homes, take to underground shelters surrounded by their surviving possessions. The fact that civilian morale did not collapse under such pressure did much to negate the Luftwaffe's efforts.

5 Coventry, 15 November 1940. Of all the provincial cities, Coventry experienced the most damaging single attack in 1940, suffering 554 civilian deaths in a 10-hour raid on the night of 14/15 November.

6 Civilians in London took to the Tube stations at night to escape the bombing. Although there were instances of people refusing to come to the surface even after the bombers had gone, in most cases morale remained remarkably high and normal city life continued.

7 Above ground, the rescue services did sterling work, digging people out of bombed buildings, often in the most difficult circumstances. In this case the rescue has taken until the following morning to complete.

8 The biggest danger in any air raid was not from high explosives but from incendiary bombs. Fire-fighting services were therefore essential and, as the night raids intensified in late 1940, they faced a difficult and dangerous task.

Chapter 2
North Africa and the Balkans 1940-42

1 General Erwin Rommel (centre) meets Italian officers on his arrival in Tripoli, February 1941. Rommel's career, beginning in World War I and ending in suicide in October 1944, was one which caught the public imagination in both Allied and Axis states, particularly during the Desert War of 1941–43.

Italy's entry into the war on 10 June 1940, closely followed by the fall of France, had left Britain's position in the Mediterranean dangerously exposed. Air attacks on Malta, initiated on 11 June, were clearly designed to sever the line of communication between Gibraltar and Egypt, and once the French fleet (elements of which were destroyed by the Royal Navy at Mers el Kébir and Dakar in early July to prevent their use by the enemy) ceased to operate in the western Mediterranean, Britain faced a loss of naval supremacy. In August control of the southern approaches to the Suez Canal was threatened by an Italian conquest of British and French Somaliland and a month later 250,000 troops under Marshal Graziani advanced out of Libya in the direction of the Canal itself. Finally, on 28 October Italian forces from Albania invaded northern Greece, opening up the unwelcome prospect of an Axis-dominated Balkans.

But the Italians were unable to sustain their offensive. Over Malta their bombers were defeated by a handful of RAF fighters, while at sea their fleet showed a marked reluctance to face the Royal Navy. In the Balkans, Greek forces absorbed the initial attacks and turned the invaders back, pursuing them deep into Albania in early 1941. By then Graziani had suffered a similar defeat at the hands of the 36,000-strong Western Desert Force commanded by Major-General O'Connor. On 9 December 1940 Italian fortified camps around Sidi Barrani were outflanked by armour and assaulted by infantry, triggering a retreat which swiftly turned into a rout as O'Connor used the mobility of his tanks to pursue, harass and constantly outmanoeuvre the enemy force. By 9 February 1941 he had reached El Agheila in Libya, having trapped the bulk of Graziani's army at Beda Fomm three days earlier. The British victory netted nearly 130,000 prisoners; they were joined by others from Ethiopia and Somaliland, caught between converging British forces from Sudan and Kenya.

The Germans could not allow their Axis partner to be defeated. As early as December 1940 Luftwaffe squadrons began to arrive in Sicily and when they joined the assault on Malta in early 1941 the RAF faced a formidable threat. The fact that the island survived at all was due to the bravery and skill of the British pilots, but the continued weakness of the Italian Navy also contributed. Supply convoys were able to reach Malta because the enemy fleet, intimidated by an audacious torpedo-bomber attack on its anchorage at Taranto (11 November 1940) and defeated in a running battle off Cape Matapan (28 March 1941), dared not interfere. Even so, the Royal Navy could not

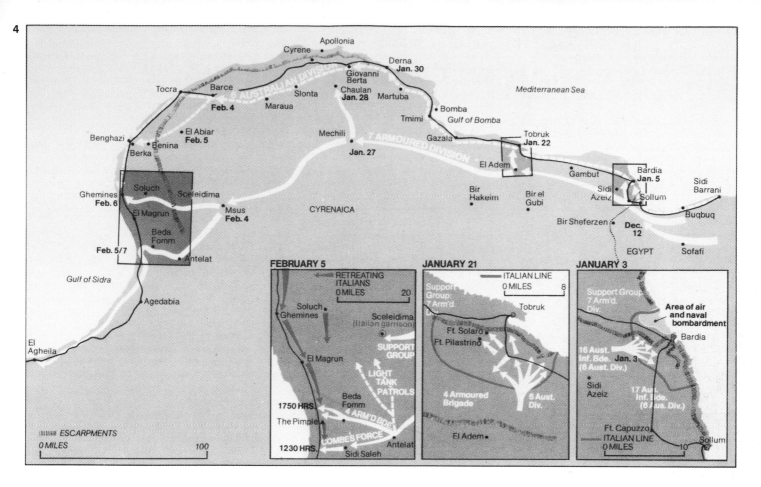

FEBRUARY 5

RETREATING ITALIANS
0 MILES 20

Soluch
Ghemines
Sceleidima (Italian garrison)
SUPPORT GROUP
El Magrun
LIGHT TANK PATROLS
Beda Fomm
1750 HRS
The Pimple
4 ARM'D BDE
1230 HRS
COMBES FORCE
Sidi Saleh
Antelat

JANUARY 21

ITALIAN LINE
0 MILES 8
Support Group: 7 Arm'd.
Tobruk
Ft. Solaro
Ft. Pilastrino
4 Armoured Brigade
6 Aust. Div.
El Adem

JANUARY 3

Support Group 7 Arm'd. Div.
Area of air and naval bombardment
Bardia
16 Aust. Inf. Bde. (6 Aust. Div.) Jan. 3
Sidi Azeiz
17 Aust. Inf. Bde. (6 Aus. Div.)
Ft. Capuzzo
ITALIAN LINE
0 MILES 10
Sollum

ESCARPMENTS
0 MILES 100

Map labels: Apollonia, Cyrene, Derna Jan. 30, Giovanni Berta, Tocra, Barce Feb. 4, Slonta, Chaulan Jan. 28, Martuba, Mediterranean Sea, Maraua, Bomba, Tmimi, Gulf of Bomba, Benghazi, El Abiar Feb. 5, Mechili, Gazala, Tobruk Jan. 22, Berka, Benina, 7 ARMOURED DIVISION, 6 AUSTRALIAN DIVISION, Ghemines Feb. 6, Soluch, Sceleidima, Jan. 27, El Adem, Gambut, Bardia Jan. 5, Sidi Barrani, El Magrun, Msus Feb. 4, CYRENAICA, Bir Hakeim, Bir el Gubi, Sidi Azeiz, Sollum, Bir Sheferzen Dec. 12, Buqbuq, Beda Fomm, EGYPT, Sofafi, Feb. 5/7, Antelat, Gulf of Sidra, Agedabia, El Agheila

---

2 Major General Leslie Morshead, Australian commander of the besieged garrison at Tobruk, 1941. Known to his troops as 'Ming the Merciless', Morshead was a tough and intelligent citizen-soldier whose actions prevented Rommel from taking Tobruk. His normal command was 9th Australian Division, which he led throughout the Desert campaign before moving on to the Southwest Pacific in late 1942.

3 The Italian dictator Benito Mussolini (left) signs the Munich Agreement, 29 September 1938, watched by the German foreign minister Joachim von Ribbentrop (right). Mussolini's subsequent adventures in North Africa and the Balkans were to drag the Germans into areas peripheral to their main strategic direction. He was killed by Italian partisans on 28 April 1945.

4 O'Connor's armoured thrust, December 1940– February 1941.

prevent the movement of German forces to Tripoli (Libya) in early February, and when the newly-formed Afrika Korps under General Rommel mounted a surprise attack on 24 March, it was soon obvious that the British had met a stronger foe. Western Desert Force, weakened by an earlier decision to send troops to Greece, withdrew leaving a garrison besieged in Tobruk.

The situation worsened when, on 6 April 1941, the Germans suddenly invaded Yugoslavia and Greece, intent upon clearing the Balkans before concentrating against the USSR. Yugoslavia, attacked by two German armies which converged on Belgrade, surrendered on 17 April; the Greeks, despite British aid, fared little better. The Metaxas Line, protecting the approaches to Macedonia in the north east, was outflanked and breached, causing the Allies to pull back down the Aegean coast. They were harried all the way by fast-moving armoured formations; by 20 April Thermopylae was threatened and six days later, after paratroops had secured the vital Corinth crossing, German units entered the Peloponnese. British troops were hurriedly evacuated, chiefly to Crete, but were pursued with vigour. On 20 May German airborne forces invaded the island, suffering heavy casualties but gradually carving out bridgeheads on the northern coast. The remnants of the British garrison were evacuated to Egypt by 31 May in an operation which cost the Royal Navy three cruisers and six destroyers.

It was fortunate that the Germans now turned towards Russia, for this allowed the British time to recover. They had already begun to consolidate their base in the Middle East – in April forces were committed to Iraq to put down a pro-Axis revolt – and this process continued with the occupation of Vichy French positions in Syria and Lebanon in June and July and a combined Anglo-Soviet operation to secure Persia (Iran) in August. By then two attempts to relieve Tobruk – Operations 'Brevity' (15 May) and 'Battleaxe' (15 June) – had failed, although Rommel's supply lines were becoming very stretched. A third British offensive, mounted by the recently-named Eighth Army under the code-name 'Crusader', began on 18 November, and after heavy fighting around Sidi Rezegh and an abortive attempt by Rommel to outflank his attackers, Tobruk was relieved. By late December the Germans had been pushed back to El Agheila.

It was now the turn of Eighth Army to suffer the effects of an over-extended supply chain, however. Rommel suddenly counter-attacked on 21 January 1942 and pushed the British back to the minefields and 'box' defences of the Gazala Line to the west of Tobruk, where both sides paused to build up supplies. It was a difficult process in which Malta, with its position astride both British and Axis communications routes, played a vital role. Throughout the first half of 1942, as Luftwaffe squadrons and German U-boats appeared in force, ferocious air and sea battles took place around the island. Not until the 'Pedestal' convoy eventually fought its way through in August, losing nine of its 13 merchantmen and four of its escorting warships on the way, did the balance tip towards the British.

Wavell's offensive
The Western Desert 1940-41

1 Italian M13/40 medium tanks in the Western Desert, 1941. Representing the best of the Italian designs, the M13/40 was reasonably well armed with a 47mm Ansaldo Model 37 main armament, backed up by three 8mm Breda Model 38 machine guns, but armour was thin and engine reliability low.

2 The most obvious result of Wavell's Offensive – a column of Italian prisoners of war, stretching as far as the eye can see. Altogether nearly 130,000 prisoners were taken in the two-month campaign. Such a haul of POWs was evidence of the rapidity of the British advance behind Italian positions.

3 A British 6in howitzer bombarding Derna, 1 February 1941. The lack of ground cover is apparent, requiring camouflage nets which gave limited protection against air observation. Fortunately for the British in early 1941, the Italian Air Force was not very effective.

4 A British ·303in Vickers machine gun lays down supportive fire from the meagre protection of a rock outcrop, January 1941. The 'smoke' is in fact steam from the water-cooling system, usually a sign that over 600 rounds have been fired in a sustained-fire pattern. The Vickers was a highly reliable machine gun capable of providing long-range supporting fire for as long as the ammunition lasted. These machine guns were typically organised as a support platoon of four or six guns, under the control of battalion headquarters.

5 Matilda II tanks of the Royal Tank Regiment, Western Desert, 1941. Designed as an infantry support tank, the Matilda was armed with a two-pounder gun which proved to be inadequate in tank-to-tank engagements, but was among the best of the tank designs available in 1940–41. Although well armoured the Matilda was unsuited to tank warfare in the desert: its snail-like maximum speed of only 13km/h (8mph) and its small calibre gun ensured that it was outclassed on the arrival of the German PzKpfw IIIs in 1941.

Abyssinia
Mussolini's empire crumbles

1 A convoy of Allied transport vehicles carries South African troops across the rolling grass lands of Abyssinia for the battles of Garai and El Guma.

2 Heavily-laden Italian troops are marshalled into line before marching off. The barrels of two 6·5mm Fiat-Revelli Model 1914 machine guns are visible as are parts of the guns' tripods.

3 The Italians faced not only the British invasion forces but locally-raised Ethiopian guerrillas, here Ras Gorussa's Patriot Army crossing a river.

4 Indian troops march against Italian positions on the Eritrean Front, 11 March, 1941.

5 British troops in an Indian brigade make use of cover while they snipe at the enemy. Armament includes .303-inch SMLE rifles and a light machine gun.

6 Ethiopian guerrillas begin their successful assault on the Italian-held fort of Delora Marcos. Under the leadership of Haile Selassie these guerrillas were a thorn in the side of the Italian armed forces.

Balkan Blitzkrieg
Yugoslavia and Greece defeated

1 Italian heavy artillery in action in Greece, November 1940.

2 A Savoia Marchetti SM-81 tri-motor bomber attacks a target in Greece, 1940. Despite the advantage of undisputed air supremacy, the Italians failed to defeat the Greeks, requiring German intervention to clear the Balkans for the Axis.

3 Italian Alpine troops – among the best soldiers available to Mussolini in 1940 – advance through mountainous terrain in Greece. It was country such as this which the Greeks were able to use to advantage, drawing the Italians into areas where the majority of their poorly trained and organised units could not operate.

4 Yugoslav troops surrender to advancing German units, April 1941.

5 German paratroopers jump from their Junkers Ju-52/3m transports over the Corinth Canal, 26 April 1941. Their seizure of vital routes over the Canal may have persuaded the German High Command to agree to the potentially risky paratroop invasion of Crete a month later.

6 A PzKpfw III Ausf E advances from Bulgaria towards Belgrade, April 1941. The flag draped over the engine compartment is for aerial recognition.

7 Greek prisoners are marched past the radio section of a Panzer regiment, April 1941. On the left stand two SdKfz 222 light armoured cars, the one to the rear converted to a command vehicle (note frame aerial); on the right is an SdKfz 232 (Fu) radio vehicle, again with frame aerial attached.

Invasion of Crete 1941

1 Major-General Bernard Freyberg VC, the commander of British forces on Crete, May 1941. Although he had a total of 30,000 Commonwealth troops (plus two ill-organised Greek divisions) in his comand, he was surprised by the German use of paratroops and forced to split his units to cover a wide range of landing zones. The Allies fought bravely but in the end were forced to withdraw. Although the Royal Navy made heroic efforts to evacuate Allied troops from Crete, over 18,000 were taken prisoner.

2 As paratroops drop to earth around Heraklion on Crete in the afternoon of 20 May, one of the transport planes is hit by ground fire. This was to be a costly campaign for the Germans – by 31 May they had lost nearly 7000 men, almost a third of their landing force.

3 Symbol of the new élite, a German paratrooper stands ready to jump from the doorway of a Junkers Ju-52.

4 General Kurt Student (centre, in peaked cap), commander of the German parachute forces, inspects a unit in distinctive paratroop garb.

5 German paratroopers regroup on their drop-zone in Crete and move off towards the enemy. A major problem for airborne forces was their shortage of heavy support weapons. The Germans attempted to make up for this by the use of lightweight mountain guns and to increase smallarms firepower through the widespread provision of sub-machine guns and, subsequently, specially manufactured assault rifles.

6 A sequence of three photographs showing civilians, accused of partisan activities, being rounded up somewhere in Crete, May 1941. Once the men had been separated from the rest, they were shot by the paratroopers. Rough justice was the order of the day whenever a region came under German control.

Rommel and the Afrika Korps

1 German artillery in action, North Africa, 1941. The gun is a 10·5cm *Leichte Feldhaubitze* 18, a World War I design which saw much service between 1939 and 1945. The exposed nature of the terrain is apparent.

2 A PzKpfw III unit deploys over level ground in Libya. It was quite unusual for tanks to appear with all the turrets closed, except in battle – the interior would soon become an intolerable furnace.

3 A PzKpfw III (this time with top turret open) closes on its target. Note the spare road wheels carried on the engine compartment – for protection as well as use in an emergency. The PzKpfw III's used in North Africa were usually equipped with the short 5cm main armament. The PzKpfw III provided the German Army in the Western Desert with an effective medium tank, even though it lacked the armour and firepower of later models.

4 German soldiers try out an
Italian mountain gun in
inappropriate terrain. The
presence of the two figures
in the background,
apparently unconcerned
about enemy action,
suggests that this is not a
battle photograph.

5 German infantry ride
through the desert on an
SdKfz 7 half-track artillery
tractor. The presence of half-
tracks in the Afrika Korps
was a bonus in the North
African terrain, providing a
ruggedness which few
Allied vehicles could match.
Beside its main function as
an artillery prime mover it
was, in addition, a useful
personnel carrier.

6 General Erwin Rommel
(second from right) confers
with the Italian Chief of
Staff, Marshal Ugo
Cavallero (centre, in
spectacles). Co-operation
between the Axis allies in
North Africa was not good
and on more than one
occasion Cavallero
demanded Rommel's recall,
but without effect. Cavallero
was to commit suicide in
August 1943, having been
accused of plotting the
overthrow of Mussolini.

Battle for Malta

1 A Savoia Marchetti SM-79 bomber of the Italian Air Force sweeps over Malta, November 1940. The clarity of view shows how vulnerable the island was to air attack and emphasises the importance of the RAF defence. By the end of the year the Italians were beginning to struggle and it was only when the Luftwaffe joined in the assault that the pressure upon Malta became acute.

2 As the pilot waits in his cockpit, armourers and fitters hurry to prepare a Spitfire for action over Malta. Ground crews in all theatres did marvellous work under often difficult conditions, but in Malta they frequently performed miracles of improvisation to ensure an air defence of the island.

3 Bombs burst among the harbour buildings of Valetta, 1941. The damage and civilian casualties inflicted upon Malta were severe, but the island did not fall. The bravery of its people was recognised by the British when the island as a whole was awarded the George Cross on 15 April 1942.

4 One of the reasons for British determination to retain Malta: the submarine base at Valetta, from which operations could be mounted throughout the Mediterranean. If Malta had fallen, these boats would have to have been withdrawn to Gibraltar or the UK, and Axis supply lines to North Africa would have become much less vulnerable.

5 The tanker *Ohio* limps into Valetta harbour, 15 August 1942, at the end of Operation 'Pedestal'. The convoy had been under constant attack since the 11th, losing nine out of 14 merchant ships, together with an aircraft carrier (HMS *Eagle*), two cruisers and a destroyer, but the arrival of the survivors, especially the *Ohio* with its cargo of precious fuel, allowed Malta to hold on.

6 Symbols of British naval strength in the Mediterranean – the aircraft carrier *Indomitable* flies off a Fairey Albacore torpedo-bomber, while *Eagle* sails behind. The photograph was taken from the deck of a third carrier, *Victorious*, with Hawker Hurricane fighters on board.

Chapter 3
From Barbarossa to Stalingrad

1 Marhsal Semyon Timoshenko, commander of the Soviet Western front and chairman of *Stavka* (the High Command) in June 1941.

2 Field Marshal von Bock (centre), commander of Army Group Centre, discusses the drive on Moscow with General Hermann Hoth (right), then commander of 3rd *Panzergruppe*. One of the most able tank generals in the Wehrmacht, Hoth later spearheaded the drive to the Caucasus.

3 General Friedrick Paulus, commander of the doomed German Sixth Army at Stalingrad, 1942–3. His surrender on 31 January 1943 (by which time he had been promoted field marshal) was a crushing blow to German morale.

4 Marshal Semyon Budenny, commander of Soviet forces in the south and southwest at the time of Barbarossa. Budenny proved a weak commander and had to be relieved in September 1941.

5 Operation Barbarossa.

The German invasion of the Soviet Union – Operation 'Barbarossa' – began at 0300 hours on 22 June 1941. Designed to destroy the bulk of Russian forces close to the border in a series of gigantic pincer movements executed by air-supported armour in classic Blitzkrieg style, the ultimate aim was to occupy Leningrad, Moscow and the Ukraine. It came very close to success.

Field-Marshal von Leeb's Army Group North, spearheaded by General Hoepner's 4th *Panzergruppe*, thrust deep into the Baltic states of Latvia, Lithuania and Estonia, capturing Daugav'pils (Dvinsk) on 26 June and crossing the Luga River to the south west of Leningrad on 14 July. By then Field-Marshal von Bock's Army Group Centre had completed a brilliant encircling move, with General Guderian's 2nd and General Hoth's 3rd *Panzergruppen* linking up to the east of Minsk on 29 June, trapping some 300,000 Russian troops in pockets around Bialystok and Gorodishche. The manoeuvre was repeated in early July towards Smolensk and when that city was reached on the 16th, von Bock had covered an incredible 580 km (360 miles) in less than a month. Only in the Ukraine, where Field-Marshal von Runstedt's Army Group South faced enormous distances and unexpected Russian counter-attacks, were the initial results less than spectacular.

Fearing Russian moves against the flanks, Hitler intervened on 19 July to divert his armour away from the drive on Moscow. Hoth was sent north to aid von Leeb and, supported by Finnish attacks from the Karelian Isthmus, Army Group North closed the ring around Leningrad in mid-September, after which siege operations began. At the same time Guderian struck south to link up with the Panzers of von Runstedt's Army Group to the east of Kiev, trapping a further 600,000 Russians by 15 September. Army Group South now forged ahead. Kiev fell on 19 September and Kharkov a month later; Romanian troops took Odessa on 16 October and two days later General von Manstein's Eleventh Army invaded the Crimea. Rostov fell on 20 November, although a combination of winter weather and inadequate supply lines forced the Germans to withdraw to the Mius River.

Nevertheless, the breakthrough at Kiev had released the Panzers for renewed operations against Moscow, initiated on 30 September. Another series of encirclements trapped substantial enemy forces around Vyaz'ma and Bryansk on 7 October and, as the citizens of Moscow hastily constructed defensive positions, the capital seemed doomed. But the Russians were helped by the weather. On 8 October autumn rains turned the ground to a quagmire and the momentum of the Blitzkrieg faltered. The Soviets, meanwhile, were pouring troops and tanks into the defence of Moscow. As the rains turned to freezing snow in mid-November, the Red Army halted the Panzers, some of which were less than 32 km (20 miles) from Red Square, and the Germans, short of fuel and ill-equipped to face a winter campaign, assumed a defensive posture. They had failed by the narrowest of margins to achieve the objective of taking Moscow.

The Russians, better prepared for the winter conditions, refused to let the invaders rest. On 6 December counter-attacks to the north and south of Moscow pushed the Germans back and Stalin ordered a more general offensive, backed by partisan activity in the enemy rear. Vast tracts of territory were liberated in January 1942, but as the Germans (under Hitler's personal direction since December) deployed into a belt of fortified 'hedgehog' positions around key locations, the campaign was not decisive. By the time of the spring thaw in March it was obvious that the Red Army could not continue its offensive.

Hitler now prepared for a summer campaign which, he hoped, would break the back of Russian resistance in the south. In May the Crimea was attacked, preparatory to an offensive by a reorganised Army Group South to capture the vital oilfields of the Caucasus. On 28 June Army Group B, comprising Fourth Panzer, Second and Sixth

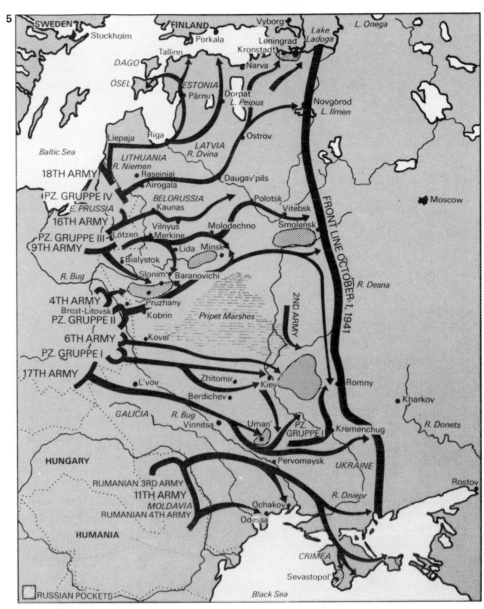

RUSSIAN POCKETS

Armies, advanced eastwards towards the Don River to establish a defensive shoulder from Voronezh to the Don Bend opposite Stalingrad which would protect Army Group A, comprising First Panzer and Seventeenth Armies, as they pushed into the Caucasus. It was to prove an overambitious manoeuvre, threatened by Russian counter-attacks from the Stalingrad salient, and although steady progress was made it soon became obvious that a change of plan was needed. On 13 July Hitler impatiently ordered Sixth Army, commanded by General Paulus, to capture Stalingrad.

Unfortunately Paulus was given inadequate armoured support – Fourth Panzer Army was sent to reinforce Army Group A on 17 July – and as a result his advance was slow. Forward units of Sixth Army managed to reach the Volga River to the south of Stalingrad on 23 August but tenacious defenders denied the Germans entry to the city itself, even after Fourth Panzer Army, in a confusing and time-consuming counter-order, was rediverted to their aid. Bitter hand-to-hand fighting developed in the western suburbs of Stalingrad, particularly around

the factory area on the river bank, and the German attacks ground to a halt. The Russians hit back on 19 November as the winter weather closed in, sending massive forces to north and south of the city in a pincer movement that all but destroyed the German satellite forces, especially the Romanian troops, holding the line there. By 23 November the whole of Sixth Army and substantial elements of Fourth Panzer Army (a total of nearly 200,000 men) were encircled and trapped.

Paulus was refused permission to break out and promised resupply by air, but as winter conditions and enemy action took a steady toll of both men and transport aircraft, his fate was sealed. An attempt by von Manstein to advance with a relieving force had failed by 23 December and Army Group A began to pull back from the potential trap of the Caucasus. On 31 January 1943 Paulus surrendered. It was a stunning blow to German morale and the turning point in the war on the Eastern Front. Before Stalingrad the Russians had enjoyed no unqualified victories; after it they were to suffer few defeats.

Barbarossa
The German invasion of Russia

1 German troops investigate the remains of a Soviet aircraft, shot down in the early days of the invasion, June 1941. As in Poland and France, the destruction of the enemy air force was an essential prerequisite of successful Blitzkrieg. In the Soviet case, however, the heavy losses did accelerate the development of new aircraft designs which, by 1943, proved a match for the Luftwaffe.

2 German infantry crouch beside a PzKpfw IV Ausf D during the initial advance into Russia, June 1941. The farm buildings on the left, having been set ablaze by tank fire, are about to be attacked. Note the extra track and road wheels carried on the tank.

3 The invaders were not always opposed. In the Ukraine, where anti-communism was deep-rooted, German soldiers were often welcomed as 'liberators' by the local people. Subsequent repressive policies in such areas were to alienate a potential source of long-term support.

4 Barbarossa was not just an armoured advance, for substantial portions of the German Army were still not mechanised. Here a cavalry unit moves eastwards in warm weather during the summer of 1941. Few of the horses were to survive the Russian winter.

5 German infantry under enemy fire – a photograph taken on 22 June 1941.

6 The value of air supremacy: Junkers Ju-87 Stuka dive-bombers, escorted by Messerschmitt Bf-109 fighters, fly unmolested over southern Russia, summer 1941. The value was to be short-lived, for although the Luftwaffe on the Eastern Front in 1941 fielded a total of 3500 aircraft, they found it physically impossible to be in all places at once. Ju-87 and Bf-109 units flew endless sorties a day but could do little to prevent the eventual recovery of the enemy air force.

Firepower and mobility
The Panzers roll east

1 The crew of a 5cm Pak38 anti-tank gun celebrate the destruction of a Soviet BT-7 tank, summer 1941. The Soviets wasted their tank potential by dissipating it in 'small packets', vulnerable to the armoured punch and anti-tank capability of the advancing German formations.

2 German infantry shelter behind a PzKpfw 35(t) during a push through close country, 1941. The 35(t) was the German version of the Czech Skoda LT-35, many examples of which had been captured in 1939 and subsequently licence-built for the German Army. Armed with a German 3·7cm KwK L/40 main gun, the 35(t) proved to be quite mobile but by 1941 it was dangerously underprotected and saw little service after 1942.

3 Red Army troops, armed with 7·62mm PPSh sub-machine guns, march through Red Square in Moscow on their way to the front line, 1941. Despite huge numbers and adequate smallarms, such troops were to be defeated and destroyed in the vast encircling battles of Barbarossa.

4 Exhausted German soldiers rest beside a PzKpfw IV during the advances of summer 1941. The Panzer formations covered enormous distances, and the wear and tear on men and machines was considerable.

5 German medical orderlies attend to a wounded soldier after what appears from the surrounding litter to have been an ambush, possibly by partisans. The wounded man has lost an arm.

6 Part of the enormous haul of prisoners taken by the Germans in 1941. Estimates vary, but it is usually accepted that well over a million Soviet soldiers were captured during Barbarossa. Few of them were to survive the rigours of four years of captivity in which they were treated as members of an inferior race and often left to starve.

Battle for Moscow
The German Army halted

1

2

1 The problems begin. A Sturmgeschütz (StuG) III with short 7·5cm L/24 gun is bogged down in mud as the autumn rains turn to snow, mid-November 1941. The vehicle in the background, with its distinctive 'G' marking, shows that this is part of *Panzergruppe Guderian*.

2 The snows caused problems for soldiers as well as vehicles – here an infantry section struggles against the wind and cold in a scene reminiscent of Napoleon's retreat from Moscow in 1812. The inadequate clothing of the Wehrmacht in 1941 is apparent.

3 Soviet troops, well-equipped against the cold, are welcomed as they liberate a village to the north of Moscow during the counter-offensive of December 1941. Such victories sustained Soviet morale at a critical time.

4 Soviet ski-troops accompany armour (a T-26 in the foreground with a T-34 behind) during the Moscow counter-attack of December 1941. Good winter clothing and superior ability to operate in snow were crucial advantages for the Soviet Army.

5 T-34 tanks, fresh from the factories, move to establish a defensive perimeter against the German advance, now fast losing momentum in the face of increasing Soviet resistance and the deteriorating weather.

4

3

5

Soviet partisans
Guerrilla war behind the lines

1 Captured partisans are executed in Minsk, 1942. The German response to partisan activities was harsh, alienating potentially sympathetic people in the occupied areas of Russia and, in many cases, provoking more determined guerrilla attacks.

2 A determined and obviously well-organised partisan group in the Smolensk area, 1943. The uniformity of dress and the fact that all seem to be armed with PPSh sub-machine guns suggests that this is a military group, organised and led by members of the Red Army.

3 A dramatic and tragic photograph, showing a member of the German armed forces firing point-blank at a woman and child, somewhere in Russia, 1942. Massacres of civilians, often perpetrated during anti-partisan sweeps, did much to increase support for the partisan groups.

4 The face of resistance – a gnarled and tough-looking partisan, armed with the ubiquitous PPSh sub-machine gun.

5 Rear-area operations by partisans could cause problems for German lines of supply and communications, as this destroyed railway bridge in southern Russia bears witness. Partisan acts were rarely this spectacular, but the threat alone was enough for the Germans to divert significant resources to the protection of their rear areas.

6 A partisan group pledges to 'defend with their last drop of blood their homeland against the German invaders'. This is probably a more typical group than that shown in photograph 2, containing women as well as men and fielding a miscellany of arms. Only the leader (probably a communist party member sent in from outside) has a PPSh.

7 German soldiers search suspected partisans during a sweep in the Orel sector, 1943. The youth of the suspects illustrates the nature of the threat to the German forces – no one, young or old, could be excluded from the searches.

Drive to the Caucasus
The German summer offensive 1942

1 The vast distances covered in the advances of 1941–42 necessitated long and wearying marches for the German infantry, but the group shown (seen here during the campaign to clear the Crimea, May–July 1942) is clearly high in morale.

2 Soviet prisoners are marched into a German position near Sebastopol in the Crimea, June 1942. Although the remnants of the Soviet garrison in Sebastopol were evacuated by sea in July, the fight for the Crimea in 1942 cost the Red Army nearly 100,000 men.

3 A photograph taken in the midst of battle: the crew of a rather exposed Pak38 anti-tank gun contribute to the destruction of Soviet armour during the Kharkov counter-offensive of May 1942. In contrast to their Soviet opponents the Germans were highly adept at combining both tank and anti-tank elements in their armoured formations.

4 A 4·7cm Panzerjaeger I in action near Rostov, July 1942. The Panzerjaeger I was the first self-propelled anti-tank gun to enter German service, being a Czech 4·7cm gun mounted on a PzKpfw I chassis and protected by a three-sided armoured gun shield. Its high silhouette made it vulnerable to counter-fire.

5 Soviet infantry advance towards a village in the Rostov area, autumn 1942. The smoke implies that there has been preliminary air or artillery bombardment.

6 A T-34 burns. The nature of the fire suggests a hit in the engine or fuel compartment, always a vulnerable part of any tank, it is unlikely that any of the crew would have survived.

5

6

Stalingrad
The Red Army Victorious

1 A German infantry section prepares for battle at the Barrikady Factory in Stalingrad, October 1942. The strain and fatigue of action is beginning to show, and these soldiers' personal weapons – Mauser M98K rifles, an MP38/40 sub-machine gun and plenty of hand grenades – reflect the nature of the relentless street fighting of the battle for Stalingrad.

2 Denied the advantage of conducting a manoeuvre battle around Stalingrad, the Germans were forced into fighting the Red Army at close range, which enabled their rugged Soviet opponents to grind them down in a battle of attrition. Here, Soviet troops adopt a typically 'heroic' pose for the camera. The two soldiers in helmets are armed with PPSh sub-machine guns, while their comrade in the side-hat is aiming a DP 1928 light machine gun.

3 Well kitted out in winter uniforms, a section of Soviet infantry prepares to close with German troops in the rubble of Stalingrad.

4 Encircled and running out of supplies, soldiers of Paulus's Sixth Army began to suffer in the ruins of Stalingrad, December 1942. The onset of winter weather added considerably to their problems and many soldiers were to die of cold and malnutrition before the surrender in early February 1943.

5 Soviet victory: a soldier raises the national flag in the ruins of a building overlooking the central square in Stalingrad, February 1943. By then the German forces in the city had lost over 100,000 dead and over 70,000 taken prisoner.

4

5

Chapter 4
Pearl Harbor and after

1 General Masaharu Homma, commander of the Japanese Fourteenth Army during the invasion of the Philippines, 1941–42. His failure to defeat the American defenders within 50 days led to his recall to Japan and he did not command in the field again. Nevertheless, he was tried (and executed) for war crimes in 1945, being held ultimately responsible for the Bataan 'Death March'.

2 The British leadership in the Far East on the eve of the Japanese attack, November 1941. Left to right: Air Marshal Sir Robert Brooke-Popham, C-in-C British Forces Far East; General Sir Archibald Wavell, C-in-C. India (recently arrived from his North African victories); Vice-Admiral Sir Geoffrey Layton, C-in-C Royal Navy, China Station.

3 General Renya Mutaguchi, commander of the Japanese 18th Division in the drive on Singapore, early 1942. Transferred to command the Fifteenth Army in Burma, Mutaguchi led the attack on British positions at Imphal and Kohima in March 1944.

At 0755 hours on 7 December 1941 Japanese torpedo-bombers spearheaded an attack upon the US Pacific Fleet at Pearl Harbor, on the Hawaiian island of Oahu. The Americans were taken by surprise, and although their aircraft carriers were fortuitously absent, the rest of the fleet was crippled. By 0945, as the last of the Japanese planes flew north to rejoin Vice-Admiral Nagumo's Strike Force carriers, five American battleships had been sunk and three others extensively damaged. The Japanese had lost only 29 aircraft in an assault which dealt a tremendous blow to American pride and prestige. The Pacific War had begun.

Japan was an expansionist, militaristic power; she had been at war with China since 1937. Denied access to strategically vital raw materials by the Western powers, who hoped to limit her military capabilities, Japan's intention now was to destroy American naval strength preparatory to the creation by conquest of a 'Greater East Asia Co-Prosperity Sphere', centred upon Malaya, the Philippines and Dutch East Indies, from which such materials could be obtained. It was hoped that the Allies, preoccupied with events in Europe, would accept the *fait accompli* and sue for peace.

The ensuing campaign was breath-taking in its speed and effects. On 8 December, as the Pearl Harbor attack was proceeding on the other side of the International Date Line, Japanese forces struck at Wake Island and Hong Kong (the garrisons surrendered on 23 and 25 December respectively), initiated air attacks on the Philippines and landed in both Thailand and northern Malaya. Bangkok was occupied on 9 December, and as the

invaders concentrated against British positions in Malaya, other units seized the Gilbert Islands and Guam. On 10 December British Naval Force Z (the battleship *Prince of Wales* and battlecruiser *Repulse*) was destroyed by Japanese aircraft off the east coast of Malaya and the invasion of the Philippines began. Six days later, landings took place in Borneo and on 22 December a large force came ashore at Lingayen Gulf to threaten Manila. Overstretched and caught by surprise, Allied units were in grave danger.

In Malaya British troops, denied air and naval support, withdrew down the peninsula to Singapore, the garrison of which surrendered on 15 February 1942. In the Philippines, American and Filipino forces under General MacArthur fared little better, holding out in the Bataan peninsula until 9 April and on the island-fortress of Corregidor until 6 May. By then the Dutch East Indies had fallen after landings in the Celebes (11 January), on Sumatra (14 February), on Timor and Bali (19/20 February) and on Java (1 March); while Burma had been invaded (15 January), initiating a British retreat which did not end until the Indian border had been reached in mid-May. Allied naval power proved ineffective – an Anglo-Dutch force which tried to protect the East Indies was destroyed on 27 February in the battle of the Java Sea – and nothing could prevent landings in New Britain (23 January) and North-East New Guinea (8–10 March). By May 1942 an enormous empire, stretching from the Kurile Islands in the north to Rabaul (New Britain) in the south, had been carved out.

4 General Hideki Tojo, prime minister of Japan, October 1941–July 1944. A leading advocate of the need for expansion and war, Tojo was tried for war crimes after the defeat of Japan and executed in 1948.

5 The Japanese assault, December 1941.

Japan's conquests were far from secure, however. The USA was certainly not disposed to seek a negotiated peace, and early in 1942 American carrier groups had begun to operate in the Pacific. On 18 April Colonel Doolittle led a bombing raid on Tokyo, using modified B-25s flown from the carrier *Hornet*. Faced with such resolve, Japanese planners instigated a second wave of attacks – towards the Aleutian Islands in the north, Midway Island in the centre and Port Moresby (Papua/New Guinea) and the Solomon Islands in the south – intended to form a protective barrier around their new possessions and to destroy the US Pacific Fleet.

In the south the Japanese invasion fleet destined for Port Moresby was intercepted by an American carrier task force, deployed to the Coral Sea on 4 May by Admiral Nimitz, commander of the Pacific Fleet. Aircraft from the rival fleets clashed on 7 and 8 May in the first of the carrier battles which were to characterise the Pacific War, and although the outcome of the Battle of the Coral Sea was a 'draw' – the Americans lost the carrier *Lexington* but destroyed its Japanese equivalent the *Shoho* – the invasion force did turn back. The Japanese then attempted an overland attack on Port Moresby, sending units to seize Buna on the east coast of Papua (21/22 July) before advancing along the Kokoda Trail across the Owen Stanley Mountains. They were opposed by Australian and American troops in some of the toughest fighting of the war

and were eventually halted only 48 km (30 miles) from their objective, on 26 September.

Meanwhile, the assault against Midway had also been contained. Aware of Japanese intentions through the breaking of their naval codes, the Americans refused to react to an attack on the Aleutians (Attu and Kiska fell on 7 June) and concentrated their forces around Midway instead. The Battle of Midway began at 0430 on 4 June 1942, and although at first American aircraft could make little headway, by mid-morning they had located and destroyed three Japanese carriers (*Kaga*, *Akagi* and *Soryu*). The Americans subsequently lost the *Yorktown*, but when a fourth enemy carrier (*Hiryu*) was crippled, Japanese naval power had been effectively blunted. It was the turning point in the Pacific campaign.

This gave the Americans the ability to intervene in the Solomons, sending Marines to destroy an airstrip being built on Guadalcanal. They landed on 7 August to face a ferocious battle which was to continue until 9 February 1943. Characterised by hard fighting in jungle terrain, the operation also saw a series of naval actions – Savo Island (8/9 August), Eastern Solomons (23/25 August), Cape Esperance (11/12 October), Santa Cruz (26 October), Guadalcanal (12/15 November) and Tassafaronga (30 November) – which gradually wore down Japanese strength. Once Guadalcanal was secure, plans for an Allied counter-offensive began.

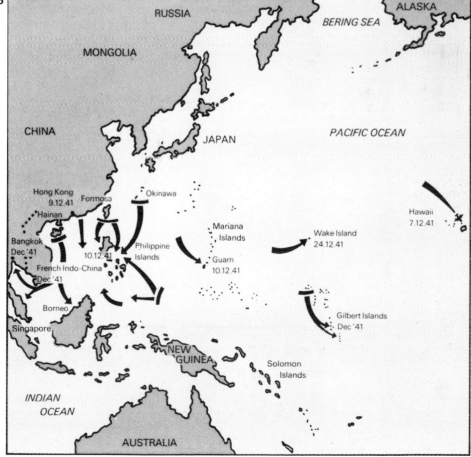

Pearl Harbor
Japan's surprise attack

1 An aerial view of Ford Island, Pearl Harbor, taken from one of the attacking Japanese planes during the first strike at 0810 hours on 7 December 1941. 'Battleship Row' may be seen on the other side of the island: the dark speck by the right-hand water spout is a Nakajima B5N torpedo-bomber (Allied code-name 'Kate') which has just hit the *Oklahoma*. The absence of American defences is apparent.

2 American naval personnel try desperately to douse fires on the *West Virginia*, mid-morning, 7 December; they could not prevent her sinking.

3 A Mitsubishi A6M Navy Type 0 carrier-borne fighter, commonly known as the 'Zero'. On 7 December 1941 the Japanese Navy deployed a total of 328 A6Ms and when they were committed to both the Pearl Harbor and Philippines attacks their manoeuvrability and range enabled them to destroy nearly all Allied air opposition. The Zero was to continue in service throughout the Pacific War, to become one of the classic fighter aircraft.

4 The remains of a B-17D Flying Fortress, destroyed by Japanese aircraft on Hickam Field, Oahu, 7 December 1941. Japanese pilots were presented with easy targets – American fighters and bombers were lined up neatly in rows, oblivious to the threat of attack. By the end of the morning of 7 December, American air power in Hawaii had been destroyed.

5 American sailors watch as the *California* gradually sinks, 7 December 1941. By 0945 the Americans had lost five battleships destroyed (*West Virginia*, *Arizona*, *Nevada*, *Oklahoma*, and *California*) and three badly damaged (*Maryland*, *Tennessee* and *Pennsylvania*). It was a crippling blow.

Japan's Blitzkrieg
The fall of Malaya and Singapore

1 Japanese troops offload supplies at one of the beach-heads during the invasion of Thailand/Malaya, 8 December 1941. Elements of the invasion fleet may be seen on the horizon.

2 British troops under Japanese guard in Singapore, 15 February 1942. Over 130,000 British and Commonwealth soldiers were taken prisoner during the Malayan campaign: all were to suffer appalling hardship during the $4\frac{1}{2}$ years of their captivity and many were to die of exhaustion, overwork and neglect.

3 Japanese Type 95 light tanks advance down a Malayan road, December 1941. Armed with a 37mm main gun, the Type 95 was mobile but poorly armoured and, given the type of terrain usually encountered, saw limited action.

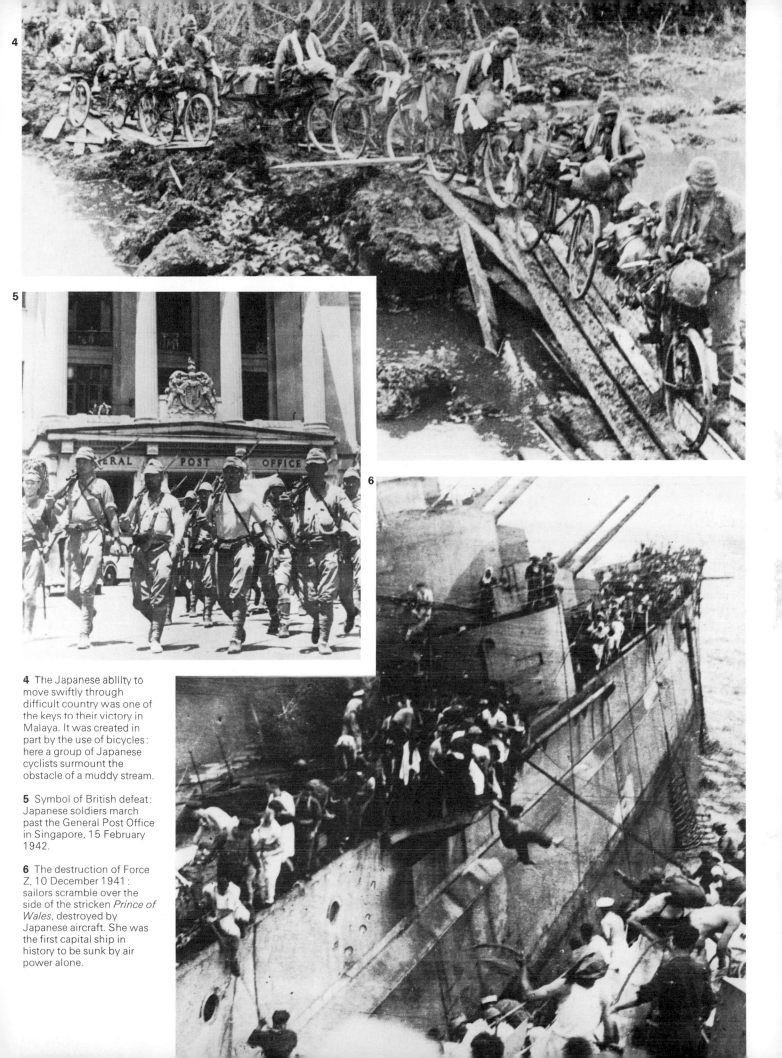

4 The Japanese ability to move swiftly through difficult country was one of the keys to their victory in Malaya. It was created in part by the use of bicycles: here a group of Japanese cyclists surmount the obstacle of a muddy stream.

5 Symbol of British defeat: Japanese soldiers march past the General Post Office in Singapore, 15 February 1942.

6 The destruction of Force Z, 10 December 1941: sailors scramble over the side of the stricken *Prince of Wales*, destroyed by Japanese aircraft. She was the first capital ship in history to be sunk by air power alone.

Bataan and Corregidor
The fall of the Philippines

1 American prisoners, captured at the fall of Bataan on 9 April 1942, march towards Camp O'Donnell at the beginning of the infamous 'Death March' (10 April to early May 1942). Of the 12,000 American and 64,000 Filipino captives who began the march, 2330 Americans and up to 7500 Filipinos died of exhaustion, dehydration and harsh treatment.

2 An American anti-tank position in the Bataan Peninsula, 1941. American troops at this stage were still wearing British-style helmets, based upon the models of World War I.

3 Japanese Marines wade ashore at Vigan on the west coast of Luzon, 10 December 1941. Members of the 'Kanno Detachment' from the Pescadores Islands, they are landing to secure an American airfield at Vigan. As the lack of opposition shown here suggests, they did not face a difficult task.

4 With Manila burning before them, Japanese soldiers prepare to land from their invasion barge. Manila was declared an open city by General MacArthur on 27 December 1941 in an effort to prevent its destruction: these troops are probably arriving to occupy the city on 2 January 1942.

5 Japanese troops select a vantage point from which to view the battle: a photograph probably taken during the initial, virtually unopposed landings on the Philippines in mid-December 1941.

6 Japanese Type 89 medium tanks cross a bridge just outside Manila, early January 1942. Armed with a 37mm main gun, the Type 89 was the main battle tank of the Japanese Army in 1941–42, but was based upon designs which were already obsolete.

Pacific turning point
Coral Sea and Midway

1 A Douglas SBD Dauntless dive-bomber leads a group of Douglas TBD Devastator torpedo-bombers of Squadron VT-5 on the deck of the carrier *Yorktown* during the Battle of the Coral Sea, early-May 1942.

2 Aichi D3A dive-bombers (Allied code-named 'Val') on board a Japanese carrier, Coral Sea, May 1942.

3 The crew of the carrier *Lexington* gather on deck before abandoning ship, 8 May 1942. The *Lexington* was hit by two bombs and two torpedoes in the late morning and was subsequently abandoned.

4 The Japanese carrier *Shoho* takes a torpedo hit from American TBD Devastators of VT-2, 1100 hours 7 May 1942.

5 SBD Dauntless dive-bombers over Midway Island, June 1942.

6 A Japanese carrier – probably the *Hiryu* – photographed from the air during the Battle of Midway, June 1942. All four Japanese carriers at Midway – *Kaga*, *Akagi*, *Hiryu* and *Soryu* – were sunk on 4 June.

7 The Japanese heavy cruiser *Mikuma*, abandoned and sinking after being hit during the Battle of Midway. She was finally sent to the bottom on 6 June by American aircraft.

8 The American carrier *Yorktown* lies dead in the water with a deep list to port, 6 June 1942: she sank the following day.

Guadalcanal
America on the offensive

1 A Japanese A6M Zero, back broken by anti-aircraft fire, goes down in flames off Guadalcanal, August 1942. The photograph, taken from the carrier *Wasp* (destined to be torpedoed and sunk on 15 September 1942) also shows part of the American invasion fleet.

2 American Marines storm ashore to the east of Tenaru, Guadalcanal, 7 August 1942. The landing was unopposed and the Marines (of 1st and 5th Marine Regiments) pushed on to take Henderson Field the following day.

3 SBD Dauntless dive-bombers on Henderson Field, Guadalcanal, December 1942. By this time the main battles had been fought and the Japanese were withdrawing westwards towards Cape Esperance and eventual evacuation. Aircraft would not have been deployed so openly while there was any chance of direct Japanese attack.

4 Japanese sailors on Guadalcanal man a 7·7mm Type 92 heavy machine gun, probably before the arrival of American Marines on 7 August 1942. The Type 92, christened the 'Woodpecker' by Allied troops because of its distinctive sound, saw widespread service in the Pacific War.

5 American aircraft attack Japanese shipping in Torolei harbour, Bougainville, 13 October 1942. As bombs burst around the seaplane tender *Akitushima*, a Mitsubishi A6M3 Zero Model 32 (allied code-name 'Hamp') is caught in the camera. Allied anti-shipping strikes in the Solomons proved to be particularly effective.

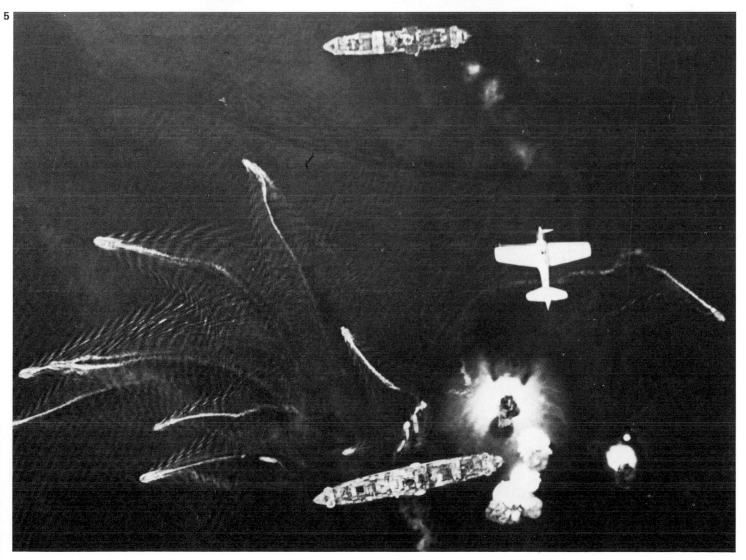

New Guinea

1 Australian soldiers with a group of New Guinea tribesmen, Huon Peninsula, 1943. They proved to be particularly useful as trackers and supply-carriers in the difficult terrain of New Guinea.

2 B-25 Mitchell medium bombers of the US 5th Air Force drop 'parafrag' (parachute-retarded fragmentation) bombs onto a Japanese airstrip, northern New Guinea, March 1944. The aircraft on the ground are Kawasaki Ki-61 fighters (Allied code-name 'Tony') of either 68th or 78th *Sentai* (squadron).

3 An Australian mortar crew prepares to fire into Japanese positions around Gona, December 1942. The weapon is a 3-inch medium mortar.

4 An American patrol, faces covered with mosquito nets, advances through relatively thin jungle, New Guinea, 1942.

5 Japanese troops defend a jungle location, New Guinea, 1943. The soldier in the centre is preparing to fire an 81mm Type 97 infantry mortar, sometimes known to the Allies as a 'knee mortar' in the belief that it was braced against the leg when fired. Anyone foolish enough to try this predictably broke his thigh. The other soldiers are armed with the standard Japanese rifle of World War II – the 6·5mm Type 38 Arisaka. The Arisaka round was low-powered and lacked accuracy.

6 The Allied counter-offensive in New Guinea – men of the US 503rd Parachute Regiment land at Numfoor, a small island off the north-east coast of Dutch New Guinea, 2 July 1944. The operation, designed to seize the Kamiri airstrip (as shown) was one of a series of amphibious and airborne landings which cleared Hollandia by the middle of 1944.

3

4

5

6

Chapter 5
Victory in North Africa

1 General Sir Bernard Law Montgomery, commander of the British Eighth Army in North Africa and Italy, 1942–43. The most famous (and controversial) British general of World War II, Montgomery breathed new life into the Eighth Army on his arrival in August 1942 and won the decisive battle of El Alamein, August–October 1942.

The rival forces in North Africa faced each other across the Gazala Line for three months (February–May 1942), building up supplies and preparing for the next round of fighting. It began on 26 May when Rommel, using part of the Afrika Korps as a diversion in the north, committed his armour to an outflanking move in the south, skirting Free French defences at Bir Hakeim before driving up behind the British positions. Eighth Army units counterattacked to prevent a breakthrough to the coast, but were unable to provide a decisive response, allowing Rommel to regroup in the 'cauldron' on 30 May, with his back to the minefields of the Gazala Line. As German engineers toiled to clear a supply route from the west, the British proved incapable of organising a counter-offensive and once Bir Hakeim had fallen (11 June), Rommel was free to break out, swinging south and then east in a move which forced the British to withdraw. By 18 June the Afrika Korps was at the gates of Tobruk (the garrison surrendered on the 21st) and on 26 June British defences at Mersa Matruh were successfully outflanked. The Eighth Army fell back to El Alamein, only 96 km (60 miles) from Alexandria.

Rommel maintained his momentum, attempting to outflank the new British defences as soon as he located them, but he was held on the Ruweisat Ridge in the first battle of Alamein (1–22 July) and soon began to run short of fuel and supplies. As the Eighth Army, commanded from 8 August by General Montgomery, was now receiving priority supplies along very short routes from the Canal Zone, the balance of forces was beginning to tilt. A second attempt by Rommel to break the Alamein Line was held on the Alam Halfa Ridge (30 August–2 September), and Montgomery prepared to counter-attack.

He was faced with a formidable task, for although Eighth Army strength had been vastly increased (by late October it comprised 195,000 men, 1029 tanks and 2311 artillery pieces, compared to the 104,000 men, 489 tanks and 1219 guns of the Axis forces), the only way to break out of a line which had no open flanks was by frontal assault. At 2130 hours on 23 October a massive artillery bombardment presaged Operation 'Lightfoot', spearheaded by infantry units of XXX Corps whose task it was to clear two corridors through the minefields in the

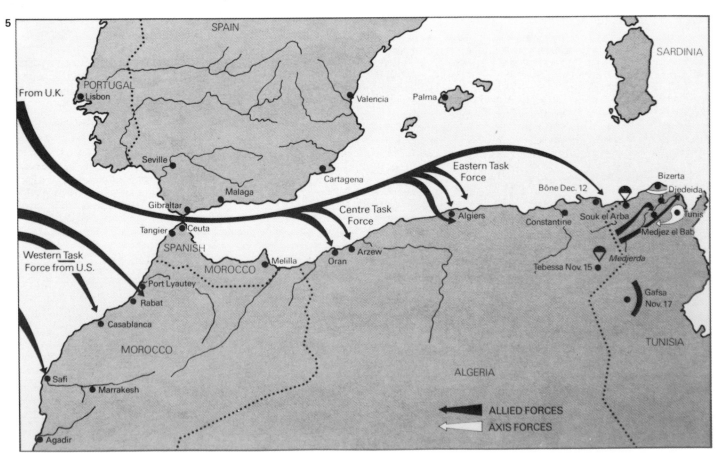

2 Rommel (right) confers with Field Marshal Albert Kesselring, C-in-C South, Tunisia 1943. Kesselring – a Luftwaffe general – was appointed to command all German forces in the Mediterranean in October 1942 and Rommel came under his jurisdiction when the Afrika Korps entered Tunisia in early 1943

3 Allied commanders meet in Tunisia, late 1942. From left to right: General Sir Harold Alexander, British C-in-C Middle East; General Dwight D. Eisenhower, Allied C-in-C Northwest Africa; General George S. Patton Jr, commander of the Western Task Force during Operation Torch.

4 General Rudolfo Graziani, appointed minister of defence in September 1943, at a time when Mussolini's power was waning.

5 Operation Torch.

Only on 2 November, as British forces concentrated against the weaker Italian sector of the enemy line in Operation 'Supercharge', was a real breakthrough achieved. Two days later, Rommel disengaged, having lost nearly 50,000 men and the bulk of his armour. By comparison, Montgomery had lost 13,500 men and retained a viable tank force.

On 8 November Rommel's position was further undermined by Anglo-American landings to his rear in French North Africa (Operation 'Torch'). Vichy units put up some resistance, but a ceasefire on the 11th gave the Allies possession of Morocco and most of Algeria. Unfortunately, Tunisia could not be secured before German troops arrived from Sicily, and although British and American paratroops tried to seize the main routes across the Algerian border, by 16 November a front had begun to harden in hilly terrain to the west of Tunis. Rommel was sufficiently alarmed, however, to pull back rapidly along the Libyan coast. By 23 November Eighth Army had reached Agedabia and two months later Tripoli was captured. The British crossed into southern Tunisia on 4 February 1943, advancing swiftly towards Rommel's last line of defence at Mareth. By then their supply line was hopelessly over-extended and Montgomery was forced to halt.

This gave Axis forces an opportunity to concentrate against the Allies' First Army (commanded by General Anderson) in a surprise attack designed to drive a wedge through the Kasserine-Tebéssa sector towards the coast. It began at 0400 hours on 14 February, catching American forces unawares and threatening to cut them off. As they withdrew on the 16th, Rommel captured Kasserine and advanced towards Le Kef. Allied reserves were hurriedly committed and, as they engaged overstretched enemy forces, Rommel was forced to withdraw. He immediately turned south, hoping to surprise Montgomery at Mareth, but despite some success on 6 March, the Eighth Army was able to defend its positions. Montgomery switched neatly to the offensive, sending forces to the left of the Mareth Line, aiming to break out of the Tebaga Gap into open ground beyond. The plan worked and by 27 March the Germans were in full retreat. It proved to be Rommel's last battle in North Africa; he was recalled to Germany a few days later.

By mid-April, therefore, Axis forces were contained in a small coastal pocket, protected by the last of the hill-lines in front of Bizerta and Tunis. The Allies concentrated in the north and centre, where features such as Hill 609 and 'Longstop' dominated key valleys. The fighting was harsh and initial attacks on 22 April failed; it was only when the Americans broke through towards Bizerta in the north on 6 May that Axis defences collapsed. Twenty-four hours later both Tunis and Bizerta fell. By 12 May all resistance had ceased. As Allied forces cleared the Cap Bon peninsula, over 250,000 Axis troops surrendered, with only a few escaping to Sicily amidst air battles which destroyed over 100 Ju-52 transport planes. The North African campaign was over.

centre, along which the armour of X Corps would pass. All elements would then concentrate on breaking through the Axis defences, after which the armour could deploy onto open ground. It proved to be a tough proposition, for although the minefields were breached by dawn on 24 October, the armour found it difficult to deploy and for nearly 10 days a bitter attritional battle had to be fought.

Gazala
War in the desert 1942

1 South African troops, armed with grenades and ·303-inch Lee-Enfield No. 4 Mark I rifles, clear a building in Sollum, January 1942, during mopping-up operations after Operation Crusader. Units of the 1st and 2nd South African Divisions, helped by British tanks, were responsible for clearing both Bardia and Sollum before advancing to take their places in the Gazala Line defences and Tobruk respectively. The surrender of Tobruk, with its substantial South African garrison, has tended to overshadow the significant contribution made by these troops to eventual victory.

2 A British 25-pounder gun-howitzer fires at enemy positions during the fighting around 'Knightsbridge' in the battle of Gazala. Robust and easy to use, it was capable of sending its 11·3kg (25 lb) shell to ranges of 12,250m (13,400 yds).

3

3 A German 8·8cm anti-aircraft gun is fired in the ground-support role something at which it proved to be extremely adept, particularly against armour. First used in this role during the Battle of France in 1940, the '88' rapidly gained an awesome reputation as an anti-tank weapon, making full use of the open spaces of the desert to engage and destroy British armour at ranges beyond those of existing tank guns.

4 American-built M3 medium tanks – known to the British as Grants – advance during the Gazala battle, June 1942. The M3 was unusual in having two guns – a useful 75mm in the side sponson and a 37mm in the turret – and its arrival in North Africa in early 1942 gave the British an advantage in firepower.

The Long Range Desert Group

1 A three-jeep SAS patrol, North Africa, 1942. The SAS, raised by Major David Stirling in November 1941 as 'L Detachment of the Special Air Service Brigade', was used principally for deep-penetration raids on enemy airfields and rear-area installations. Wearing Arab head-dress and invariably bearded, the men traversed the desert in specially-converted jeeps or trucks, well-protected by machine guns.

2 Side view of a typical SAS jeep, equipped for long-range penetration work. In this particular case, a ·50-inch machine gun is mounted on the hood, with twin ·30-inch mountings on front and rear. The jerricans, spare wheels and personal packs make for a crowded vehicle.

3 An SAS patrol gets under way. Working in conjunction with the Long Range Desert Group (LRDG), such patrols, operating out of Kufra and the Qattara Depression, carried out some 20 deep-penetration raids between December 1941 and March 1942, destroying 115 enemy aircraft and numerous vehicles.

4 A Chevrolet truck, armed with a Lewis gun (left) and ·50-inch Browning, of the LRDG, North Africa, 1941. Formed in 1940 to watch Italian outposts in southern Libya, the LRDG comprised volunteers with experience in desert travel and conditions, but it was not long before they took the offensive, initially in conjunction with Free French units from Chad and then, after November 1941, with the newly-formed SAS. The LRDG was usually responsible for guiding the SAS to their targets rather than for the attacks themselves.

5 An LRDG patrol moves out of Cairo, September 1942, aboard their Chevrolet trucks. This photo was taken at the time of the combined SAS/LRDG raids against Barce, Benghazi and Tobruk – elaborate affairs in which, however, security was poor and the success rate low.

1

2 **3**

El Alamein
Eighth Army triumphant

1 A Curtiss P40N – known in RAF service as the Kittyhawk IV – of No. 112 Squadron, RAF, taxies for take-off on a desert airstrip, October 1942. The squadron, famous for its distinctive 'shark's teeth' markings, was responsible for helping maintain air superiority over the battle area.

2 The British preliminary night bombardment, Alamein, 23 October 1942. This was the largest artillery barrage of the desert war, delivered by over 1000 field and medium guns. The photograph shows a 25-pounder gun-howitzer – the mainstay of British field artillery units throughout World War II.

3 An officer, with pistol drawn, leads his men forward. Despite large numbers (70,000 men, backed by 600 tanks), the infantry attack at Alamein soon bogged down into hard attritional fighting.

4 PzKpfw IIIs, with 5cm main armament, occupy exposed positions, Alamein front, 1942.

5 American-built M4 medium tanks, more commonly known as Shermans, advance to make contact with the Afrika Korps, early-November 1942. The armour break-through, achieved after heavy fighting in Operation 'Supercharge', was the key to British victory at Alamein.

6 A British soldier advances with bayonet fixed towards a knocked-out German PzKpfw III.

5

6

1 American and French officers confer, Northwest Africa, 1942. Despite the cooperation here implied, the Anglo-American invaders initially received little help from the pro-Vichy garrisons and fighting took place around all three landing areas – Casablanca, Oran and Algiers – before a ceasefire could be arranged.

2 American infantry come ashore in the Gulf of Arzew, east of Oran, 8 November 1942. Part of the Central Task Force under Major General L. R. Fredenhall, these troops enjoyed a virtually unopposed landing but encountered heavy resistance from French defenders as they pushed inland.

3 The propaganda image of 'Torch' – US troops advance behind the flag towards the Maison Blanche airfield outside Algiers, 8 November 1942.

4 American artillery is pulled ashore, Operation 'Torch', 8 November 1942. The lack of enemy action and the presence of British troops implies that this is an Eastern Task Force beach at Algiers.

5 American troops approach the Algerian shore-line in British-manned landing craft, 8 November 1942. Note the Stars and Stripes recognition arm-band on the soldier at the rear of the boat.

6 An American soldier takes position on a rooftop in Oran, 10 November 1942. Once the town had been secured, members of the Central Task Force pushed eastwards to link up with units of the Eastern Task Force at Algiers.

Battle for Tunisia
Germany's defeat in North Africa

1 Troops of the British First Army enter Tunis in triumph, 7 May 1943. The relief after six months of hard fighting is apparent.

2 A dramatic and unusual shot of an air-to-air battle in progress over the Sicilian Narrows, early-May 1943. As Axis forces are withdrawn from Tunisia, Junkers Ju-52 transports, hugging the wave-tops in an effort to escape detection, are shot out of the sky by B-25 Mitchell bombers (top left) and P-38 Lightning fighters. In this particular case, 25 of the 35 Ju-52s encountered were destroyed.

3 British troops fire a PIAT (projector, infantry, anti-tank) at the burning hulk of a PzKpfw IV, Tunisia, 1943. The PIAT was a fairly simple projector, launching a 1·4kg (3lb) hollow-charge projectile by means of an enormous spring. Effective range was about 91m (100 yds), but accuracy was not guaranteed. The weapon was heavy – 14·5kg (32lb) – required two men to fire it and was renowned for its violent kickback, but it constituted a useful first experiment in infantry anti-tank defence.

4 A PzKpfw III Ausf J in Tunisia, 1943. Still armed with the short 5cm main armament, the PzKpfw III was by now dangerously vulnerable to up-gunned Allied tanks and anti-tank weapons.

5 An American M5A1 light tank – known to the British as the Stuart IV – advances through semi-desert terrain in Tunisia, 1943. The M5, with its 37mm main gun, was not a great deal of use in tank-to-tank engagements, but it proved valuable for reconnaissance and flank protection, tasks it was to carry out in US armoured divisions until the end of the war. In this photograph the M5 is followed by a jeep and an M3 half-track, both useful vehicles in North Africa, as elsewhere.

Chapter 6

The Battle of the Atlantic

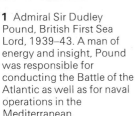

Great Britain depended for her survival upon maritime trading routes. Between September 1939 and May 1943 she faced the prospect of defeat almost daily as German submarines (U-boats), warships, merchant raiders and aircraft tried to sever such routes, particularly those across the North Atlantic. If they had succeeded, Britain would have been forced to surrender to avoid starvation and the Allies would have lost the base from which to mount a land campaign in western Europe. Winston Churchill recalled that 'the Battle of the Atlantic was the only thing which really worried me during the war', and it is not difficult to see why.

The threat became apparent as early as 3 September 1939, when the passenger-liner SS *Athenia* was sunk by a U-boat, and during the next few days a further 27 merchant ships suffered the same fate. Convoys were introduced by the Admiralty on 7 September, but with only 26 escort warships available and a lack of air cover beyond the range of shore-based aircraft, they were not particularly effective. Although the Germans could deploy only 22 ocean-going submarines when war broke out, the techniques of convoy protection were poor and U-boat captains, avoiding detection by attacking on the surface at night, soon exploited British weaknesses. Nor did the situation improve in 1940, for the naval losses incurred by Britain in the battles for Norway and France, combined with an inability to build ships as fast as they were being sunk, merely exacerbated the problem. A deal with the United States in September produced 50 aged destroyers in exchange for the leasing of British bases in Newfoundland and the Caribbean, but with the Germans occupying ports in Europe which were close to the Atlantic sea-lanes, the U-boats enjoyed their 'Happy Time'. By the end of 1940 over 1200 merchant ships, equivalent to more than a quarter of Britain's pre-war mercantile marine, had been destroyed.

But the U-boats were not the only menace, for during the same period German warships regularly prowled the oceans. The first were the battleships *Graf Spee* and *Deutschland*, already at sea when war was declared. *Deutschland* enjoyed little success, returning to Germany on 1 November, but *Graf Spee* spread fear and confusion throughout the South Atlantic. On 13 December 1939 she was caught and damaged by three British cruisers off the River Plate and forced to retire to the neutral port of Montevideo for repairs. Four days later, unable to abuse neutrality any longer and unwilling to face a British fleet offshore, her captain scuttled her. It was a welcome boost to British morale, although it did nothing to prevent other warship sorties. The battleships *Scharnhorst* and *Gneisenau* ventured out in November 1939, February 1940 and January-March 1941, while the *Admiral Scheer* spent five months at sea between November 1940 and March 1941. The presence of these powerful warships forced the Royal Navy to disperse its defence effort, leaving merchantmen poorly protected against U-boats (which now concentrated upon selected convoys in 'Wolf Packs') and against disguised merchant raiders.

1 Admiral Sir Dudley Pound, British First Sea Lord, 1939–43. A man of energy and insight, Pound was responsible for conducting the Battle of the Atlantic as well as for naval operations in the Mediterranean.

2 Captain R. St V. Sherbrooke VC, one of the most successful escort commanders of the Atlantic battles. Responsible for protecting convoy JW 51B (the first of the Arctic convoys after PQ 18) in December 1942, Sherbrooke pitted his force of six destroyers against the German capital ships *Hipper* and *Lützow* in the Barents Sea (31 December). Despite being wounded, he directed the battle from HMS *Onslow* and forced the enemy to withdraw. His Victoria Cross was richly deserved.

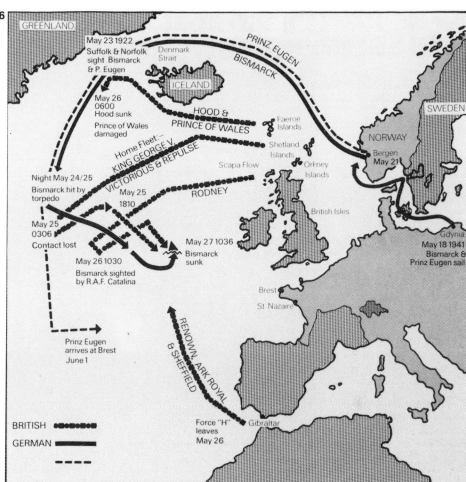

3 U-boat crews listen attentively as Admiral Karl Doenitz, their C-in-C, addresses them at Kiel, 1942. Doenitz was responsible for the conduct of the U-boat war and, appointed C-in-C of the German Navy in March 1943.

4 Grand Admiral Erich Raeder (right) C-in-C of the German Navy 1928–43, on board the warship *Gneisenau*, 1941. Raeder had directed the rebuilding of the German fleet between the two world wars, and when Hitler ordered its virtual disbandment in favour of U-boats in 1943 – after the disastrous battle of the Barents Sea – Raeder resigned.

5 Captain Gunther Prien brings *U-47* into harbour at the end of a successful voyage in the Atlantic. A U-boat ace, Prien penetrated British defences at Scapa Flow on 13/14 October 1939 and torpedoed the battleship *Royal Oak*.

6 The hunt for the *Bismarck*.

What success the British did enjoy came slowly and at some cost. The warship threat was gradually contained, with the destruction of the battleship *Bismarck* on 27 May 1941 after a chase in which the battlecruiser HMS *Hood* was lost, and the sinking of two merchant raiders, *Kormoran* and *Atlantis*, in November. At the same time convoy protection improved, based upon the advantages of sonar, radio intercepts and more effective depth-charges, although the U-boats remained elusive, with only 24 being destroyed in 1941. The deployment of long-range aircraft to bases in Canada, Greenland and Iceland began to plug the 'air gap', and in December 1941, with the introduction of specially-built escort carriers, air protection became available all the way across the Atlantic. Finally, the entry of America into the war provided an immediate reinforcement to the escort fleet and promised a virtually unlimited ship-building capacity, although to begin with the U-boats enjoyed another 'Happy Time' among the unprotected coastal shipping of the eastern seaboard.

Meanwhile the British faced yet another crisis, this time in the Arctic as they delivered Lend-Lease supplies to Russia. At first all went well – between September 1941 and February 1942 only one ship was lost – but as the Germans moved warships, aircraft and U-boats against the 'PQ' convoys, merchant losses increased, culminating in July 1942 with the disaster that befell convoy PQ 17, when 22 supply ships were sunk. PQ 18 in Sep-

tember fared little better, losing 13 vessels, and the convoys had to be suspended. When they were resumed in December, improved tactics and stronger escorts gradually gained the upper hand, although it took the crippling of the battleship *Tirpitz* by X-craft (September 1943) and the sinking of the *Scharnhorst* in the battle of North Cape (December 1943) before victory could be assured and the supply-lines to the Soviet Union maintained on a regular basis.

By then the crisis in the Atlantic had been reached. Despite a steady rise in U-boat losses (87 in 1942), the pressure on the convoys continued, culminating in March 1943 when 82 ships were sunk in the Atlantic alone. Britain stood perilously close to starvation and, as U-boat deployment reached 240 in April, it was clear that a decisive confrontation was imminent. It came in May when, in a series of hard-fought convoy battles, 41 U-boats were destroyed for the loss of only 34 merchant ships. A combination of effective escort tactics, improved radar and air cover had given the Allies a crucial advantage and, as American shipbuilding began to outpace the losses incurred, the Atlantic sea-lanes became less dangerous. Attacks on convoys continued, although with U-boat losses of 237 in 1943 and 242 in 1944, Allied victory was undeniable. The cost had been high – by 1945 Britain had lost over 5000 merchant ships – but the results were decisive. Victory in the Atlantic was an essential prelude to victory in Europe.

The U-boat threat

1 A U-boat travels on the surface towards its hunting grounds in the North Atlantic, 1940.

2 U-boats in the Baltic conduct 'shake-down' exercises preparatory to commitment to the Atlantic battle. Some 1162 U-boats were built between 1939 and 1945, of which the majority – over 700– were Type VIIs. With a range of 6500 nautical miles (at 12 knots) and a surface speed of 17 knots, they could move far and wide over the Atlantic sea lanes.

3 A U-boat crew member on the deck of his submarine in rough waters. The standard-fit 8·8cm deck gun is shown, although in many instances U-boat captains had these removed and replaced with 2cm anti-aircraft cannon in double or quadruple mountings – a sure sign that the air threat was the one most feared.

4 The chief engineer officer of a U-boat shows how cramped the conditions were on board. On a normal cruise, the crew could expect to be living in such conditions for up to four months, with few opportunities for fresh air.

5 The commander of a U-boat, wearing the distinctive white cap-top, uses his periscope to search for enemy shipping. The buccaneer spirit of many U-boat commanders – particularly the 'aces' such as Otto Kretschmer, Joachim Schepke and Gunther Prien – ensured them a place in German wartime propaganda, but few were to survive. By May 1945 the Germans had lost 781 U-boats and 32,000 submariners in the Battle of the Atlantic.

6 A U-boat stands by as survivors from a British merchant ship row over. In the early stages of the Atlantic battle, it was not unusual for the U-boats, having attacked their victims on the surface, to stand by to pick up survivors.

7 A merchantman sinks – a photograph taken from the deck of the attacking U-boat.

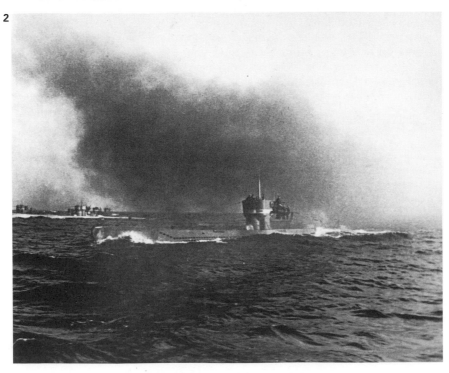

5

6

7

The convoy war

1 A British merchantman – the SS *Coulmore* – weathers an Atlantic storm, early 1943. In addition to the threats from enemy submarines, surface ships and aircraft, the convoys had also to face atrocious weather conditions, especially on the Arctic 'run' to Russia.

2 The horrors of the convoy war: the Russian tanker *Azerbaijan* is hit by a torpedo during the early attacks on Convoy PQ 17, 4 July 1942. Setting out from Iceland on 27 June, PQ 17 consisted of 35 merchant ships with a close escort of 19 Royal Navy vessels. Ordered to 'scatter' late on 4 July when it was thought that German capital ships in Norwegian waters were about to mount an attack, 24 of the merchantmen were picked off by air and submarine action over the next few days. It was a bitter blow.

3 An Atlantic convoy nears home waters, 1943. The size and shape of a typical convoy may be seen from this photograph, taken from a Coastal Command Flying Fortress. The provision of adequate escorts and long-range air cover, implicit in this view, were the keys to allied victory.

4 An escort warship rushes round a convoy as one of the merchantmen is hit. The escorts, despite a shaky start when so few were available, did sterling work throughout the battle for the sea-lanes, keeping the convoys together and creating at least a potential for protection from air and submarine attack.

5 The crew of a German warship watch as a merchant ship sinks. Although the majority of British merchant losses were to submarines or air attack, surface ships – whether disguised merchant raiders or conventional warships – did venture out to disrupt the sea-lanes.

3

4

5

The voyage of the Bismarck

1 The British battlecruiser
HMS *Hood*, sunk by the
Bismarck on 24 May
1941. when *Bismarck*,
accompanied by the heavy
cruiser *Prinz Eugen*, was
sighted in the Skagerrak on
20 May, the British hurriedly
despatched a naval force –
the battleships *Prince of
Wales* and *King George V*,
battlecruiser *Hood*, aircraft
carrier *Victorious*, four
cruisers and nine destroyers
– to intercept. The enemy
ships were next sighted in
the Denmark Strait late on
the 23rd and the British
attacked at 0522 hours on
the following day. *Hood*
blew up only eight minutes
later, hit by a salvo from
Bismarck; three members of
her crew of 1419 survived.
But *Bismarck* had been
damaged, forcing her
captain to head for the safety
of Brest.

2 The battleship *Bismarck*
leaves the Baltic, May 1941.
Laid down in 1936 and
launched by Hitler three
years later, *Bismarck* was a
formidable warship,
mounting eight 38cm (15-
inch) main guns and a
secondary armament of
twelve 15cm (5·9-inch)
weapons, together with an
array of anti-aircraft guns
and two Arado Ar-196
seaplanes.

3 Fairey Swordfish torpedo-
bombers, of the type which
attacked the *Bismarck* on
two occasions in May 1941.
On the first, Swordfish from
the carrier *Victorious* located
the battleship late on
24 May but failed to score
any direct hits; two days
later similar aircraft from the
Ark Royal succeeded in
damaging *Bismarck*'s
steering, leaving the ship
vulnerable to the converging
British fleet.

4/5 Two views of *Bismarck*
firing broadsides with her
38cm (15-inch) main
armament.

6 Survivors from the
Bismarck are picked up by
the cruiser HMS
Dorsetshire, 27 May 1941.
Once damaged by
Swordfish attack, *Bismarck*
could not avoid the British
fleet. Early on 27 May the
battleships *King George V*
and *Rodney* pounded her
mercilessly before calling in
the *Dorsetshire* to finish her
off with torpedoes. Only 110
of *Bismarck*'s crew survived.

Anti-submarine warfare

1 Depth-charges are dropped from the stern of the escort destroyer HMS *Skate*. Developed in World War I, depth-charges were steel-cylinders filled with Amatol or TNT, released from the hunter vessel with a pre-set hydrostatic pistol which detonated the main charge at the depth which the submarine was reckoned to be. Pressure waves could stove in a U-boat hull at 15m (50 ft), but this required an accuracy which could not always be guaranteed. With the development of ASDIC detection devices the situation improved.

2 A British escort warship engages German aircraft on the Arctic 'run' to Russia, 1942. The air threat was a considerable one, with German bombers stationed in northern Norway able to catch the convoys as they were forced within range by the proximity of the ice-cap.

3 A 'Hurricat' – Hawker Sea Hurricane IA – is launched from a rocket-assisted hydraulic catapult on board a CAM (catapult aircraft merchantman) ship. A stop-gap measure designed to provide urgently-needed cover for merchant ships beyond the range of shore-based aircraft, the CAM conversions were never particularly popular with the pilots, as they had to ditch alongside the parent ship in the hope of being picked up.

4 Short Sunderland long-range flying boats were used throughout the Battle of the Atlantic for reconnaissance, anti-submarine warfare and convoy protection. The photograph shows the late-development Mark V version, powered by four American 1200hp Pratt and Whitney Wasp R-1830 radial engines and carrying ASV (air-to-surface vessel) radar.

5 The destroyers HMS *Onslow* (foreground) and *Ashanti*, typical of the escort warships available to the Royal Navy during the war years.

3

4

5

Sinking the Tirpitz

1 An exceptionally clear aerial shot of the battleship *Tirpitz*, lying in Narvik-Bogen Fjord, July 1942. As replenishment vessels float alongside, the sheer size of the warship may be appreciated and her eight 38cm (15-inch) main guns seen. A protective torpedo-net is denoted by the row of white dots at the bottom of the photograph. In July 1942 *Tirpitz* was posing a significant threat to the Arctic convoys; it was a rumour of her movement into the sea-lanes at this time that led to the scattering of the PQ 17 convoy, with disastrous results.

2 Fairey Albacore torpedo-bombers attack the *Tirpitz*, mid-1944. By this time the battleship had been damaged by X-type midget submarines (23 September 1943) and moved to Tromso Fjord for repairs. Torpedo-bombers managed to make some hits during attacks in April 1944, but *Tirpitz* was still capable of putting up a strong anti-aircraft defence, as shown. Even so, she was not to appear in open waters again.

3 By May 1945 the menace of German warships in Norwegian waters had been effectively countered and the Royal Navy enjoyed complete control. This photograph shows an attack by Fleet Air Arm aircraft from the carriers *Searcher*, *Queen* and *Trumpeter* on German depot ships near Narvik.

4 The hulk of the *Tirpitz*, Tromso Fjord, May 1945. She was finally destroyed by Avro Lancaster bombers of No. 617 Squadron, RAF (the 'Dam Busters') on 12 November 1944. Equipped with 5·5 ton 'blockbuster' bombs, 29 Lancasters caught the Germans by surprise, hitting the battleship three times and causing her to capsize. Over 1000 crew members were trapped in the overturned hull. It was the end of a career for the *Tirpitz* which saw little direct action but which, through presence in Norwegian waters, forced the British to divert substantial air and naval resources from other tasks.

5 *Tirpitz* lies close to the shore in Tromso Fjord, 1944. Camouflage nets may be seen on the starboard (onshore) side, ready to be pulled over the ship in the event of an air threat. With anti-torpedo nets offshore and smoke pots liberally deployed to create an instant screen, the battleshp was well-protected, requiring considerable effort on the part of the British before she could be destroyed.

Chapter 7
The Russian steamroller

1

Victory at Stalingrad in early 1943 was the signal for Soviet offensives all along the Eastern Front. Even before Paulus surrendered in late January, a series of assaults had forced Army Group A out of the Caucasus and broken through all along the German line from Orel to Rostov. By the time of the spring thaw in March the Russians had retaken Kursk and were threatening Kharkov; only in the south, where Field-Marshal von Manstein conducted a brilliant armoured counterstroke against the Russian flank beyond the Donets River, was a semblance of order retained.

But Hitler refused to face reality, believing that the Red Army was over-extended and vulnerable to counter-attack. As the summer approached, his attention turned to positions around Kursk, where the speed of Russian advance had created a large salient which invited destruction. Unfortunately German forces were in no condition to mount an immediate attack, and although the basic operational plan – 'Citadel' – was quickly formulated, delays occurred as fresh troops and the latest Mark V Panther and Mark VI Tiger tanks were delivered. This, coupled with information from the 'Lucy' spy-ring in Switzerland, enabled the Russians to anticipate the attack; when it was finally

delivered on 5 July, they were firmly established behind a formidable belt of prepared positions, in some cases to a depth of 80 km (50 miles). The intention was to blunt the impact of Blitzkrieg, enmeshing German armour in line after line of interlocking defences.

This was exactly what happened. In the north Field-Marshal von Kluge's Ninth Army made little progress, advancing less than 10 km (6 miles) by 10 July for the loss of 25,000 men and 200 tanks, and although von Manstein's Fourth Panzer Army enjoyed slightly more success, creating a wedge some 40 km (25 miles) deep in the southern sector, they too became bogged down. The Russians, commanded by Generals Zhukov and Vasilevsky, committed their armour on 12 July and in a massive battle around the village of Prokhorovka, in which an estimated 2000 armoured vehicles took part, von Manstein was defeated for the loss of 10,000 men and 350 tanks. These were unacceptable losses and, as the Red Army exploited its victory by retaking Orel and Kharkov, the Germans came close to collapse. Overwhelming Soviet forces, supported by partisans and sustained by defence industries which were now working flat out, built up a terrifying momentum all along the line from

2

3

4

5

1 Marshal Ivan Konev, appointed to command the 2nd Ukrainian Front in January 1944. Already famous for his defeat of German forces around Kursk in July 1943, Konev went on to command the 1st Ukrainian Front for the drive through Poland.

2 Marshal Konstantin Rokossovsky, commander of the 1st (and later 2nd) Belorussian Front, 1944–45. Having fought at Stalingrad and Kursk, Rokossovsky already had a fine reputation and this was enhanced by his drives towards Warsaw and Danzig in the last year of the war. However, despite his own Polish origins, it was his armies which stopped short of Warsaw in August 1944, leaving the non-communist Polish Home Army to its fate.

3 Field Marshal Erich von Manstein, often described as the finest German field commander of World War II. An early proponent of mobile warfare, he masterminded the Army Group A assault of May 1940 before seeing widespread service on the Eastern Front. In the post-Stalingrad battles of 1943 he conducted a brilliant campaign beyond the Donets River using 'mobile defence'. He was dismissed by Hitler in April 1943.

4 *SS-Obergruppenführer* (army rank–general) Erich von dem Bach-Zelewski, the man responsible for suppressing, with great brutality, the Warsaw Uprising of August 1944. Shown here in *Waffen-SS* uniform – he was chief of anti-partisan units on the Eastern Front – Bach-Zelewski went on to command XIV SS Corps in Hungary in autumn 1944.

5 Colonel General Heinz Guderian: although one of the best tank generals of the war, he was relieved by Hitler in October 1941 for questioning the supreme commander's strategy. Recalled as Inspector General of Armoured Troops in February 1943 and promoted to Chief of Staff in July 1944 he was to be dismissed again in March 1945, symbolising the waste of human potential which so often accompanied Hitler's policies.

Smolensk to Rostov. Casualties were enormous on both sides but by the end of 1943 the Russians had reached the Dniepr River, liberated Kiev and trapped the German Seventeenth Army in the Crimea.

The Russian aim in 1944 was to clear the country of all enemy troops. In the north the siege of Leningrad, which had lasted for 900 days and cost over a million civilian lives, was broken in January and Army Group North was forced to withdraw towards the Baltic states. At the same time, to the south of the Pripet Marshes, forces under Generals Zhukov, Konev, Malinovsky and Tolbukhin smashed out of positions on the Dniepr, catching the Germans off-balance and pushing them back as far as the Dniestr River. The First Panzer Army was encircled at Korsun and although most of the men escaped after heavy fighting, losses in equipment were crippling. Further south, Odessa was liberated on 10 April and the Crimea was cleared; by the end of May the Russians were approaching the borders of Poland and had actually crossed into Romania.

But the main offensive of the year was yet to come. On 22/23 June, in Operation 'Bagration', over 2,500,000 Soviet troops, supported by overwhelming artillery and armour, attacked Army Group Centre in Belorussia. It was a decisive campaign, with well-executed pincer moves trapping a total of 25 German divisions to the east of Minsk by the end of July. Army Group Centre, shocked and demoralised, could not prevent a Russian breakthrough. As Konev mounted a flank attack through L'vov to the south, Zhukov thrust deep into Poland, reaching the Vistula River opposite Warsaw just as

the Polish Home Army rose in revolt against their German oppressors. It is not clear whether the Soviet forces were incapable or unwilling to lend their support, but the advance was stopped and by early October the Poles had been crushed.

Meanwhile, further success had been achieved on the flanks. In the north the Finns were attacked in June (they agreed to an armistice three months later) and a simultaneous advance into the Baltic states trapped the remnants of Army Group North in the Kurland Peninsula by late September. By then a major offensive in the south, begun on 20 August, had pushed the Germans into the Balkans. With Russian forces on the Danube and approaching the borders of Hungary, both Romania and Bulgaria had sued for peace by early September and German units in Yugoslavia and Greece, harried by partisans, were withdrawing rapidly northwards to escape a developing trap.

The Red Army now paused to build up supplies for its next major offensive, which exploded into action all along the line, from East Prussia in the north to Jasło in the south, on 12 January 1945. Warsaw fell on 17 January and Marshals Zhukov and Rokossovsky advanced north-westwards along the Vistula, forcing Army Group Centre to withdraw to Danzig (Gdansk) by early February. Over 500,000 German troops were trapped, and although valiant attempts were made to evacuate them by sea, the losses were substantial. Meanwhile, elements of Zhukov's forces, together with Konev's to the south, swept into the gap left by Army Group Centre and by 31 January had reached the Oder River, less than 65 km (40 miles) from Berlin. The final offensive was only a matter of time.

Kursk
The greatest tank battle

1 PzKpfw V Panther tanks open the German attack at Kursk, 5 July 1943. The Panther, armed with a high-velocity 7·5cm main gun, had been developed in answer to the threat posed by the Russian T-34/76 when it was encountered in 1941.

2 PzKpfw IVs, armed with 7·5cm guns, move into position preparatory to the Kursk assault, July 1943. To provide protection against Soviet anti-tank hollow-charge projectiles, the tanks have been fitted with additional armour plates (known as *Schützen*).

3 Early production PzKpfw VI Ausf H Tiger I tanks, Kursk area, August 1943. Developed in 1942, the Tiger I was a formidable vehicle: it weighed 56 tons, was protected by up to 100mm (four inches) of armour plate and carried an 8·8cm main armament.

4 A T-34/76 burns; Kursk, July 1943. In the massive tank battles which took place around Kursk and Orel in July and early-August 1943, up to 2000 armoured vehicles were deployed. The losses were heavy on both sides.

5 T-34/76s advance under fire to engage the enemy, Kursk/Orel, July 1943. The initial German attack on the Kursk salient – Operation 'Citadel' – was absorbed by Soviet infantry and artillery in elaborate prepared defences, while the bulk of the armour was held back for a counter-stroke. When it came on 12 July, the tank battle began in earnest.

6 A PzKpfw VI Tiger, members of its crew lying dead in the foreground, stands as burning testimony to Soviet success, July 1943.

7 Soviet infantry clean their weapons – 7·62mm Mosin-Nagant 1891/30 rifles – after the Kursk battle, August 1943. Their success in denying armoured momentum to the Germans was crucial to Soviet victory.

5

6

7

The Red Army

1 Despite the success of Soviet armour in 1943, the Red Army still contained substantial numbers of horsed soldiers, useful for pursuit and reconnaissance over the open steppes of the Ukraine. Here members of General Selivanov's cavalry pursue the retreating enemy, 2nd Ukrainian Front, 1944.

2 The old and the new: as Soviet horse-drawn artillery units advance over marshy ground, Ilyushin Il-2 Shturmovik ground-attack aircraft fly overhead. The most effective Shturmovik tactic was known as the 'Circle of Death' and entailed a series of low-level attacks against a chosen target by seemingly-endless waves of circling aircraft.

3 Soviet infantry cling to the hulls of T-34s as the advance continues over flooded terrain, 1st Ukrainian Front, March 1944.

4 A Soviet political officer (commissar), badly wounded in face and head, urges his soldiers forward during the 1944 advances.

5 A Soviet 203mm howitzer Model 1931, lays down supporting fire, Ukrainian Front, 1944. The Model 1931 was the heaviest Soviet artillery piece of World War II, capable of throwing a 100kg (220lb) shell out to a range of 16,000m (17,500 yds). Its tracked chassis made it particularly useful in rugged terrain.

6 Soviet gunners soften up an enemy position, 2nd Baltic Front, 1944. The gun is a 76·2mm (3-inch) Model 1939, possessing a range of 13,250m (14,500 yds). Massive artillery barrages were a feature of Soviet attacks by 1944 – during Operation Bagration in June, a density of almost 400 guns for every mile of front was attained.

Leningrad
The brutal siege

1 Street scene in Leningrad after a German shelling of the city in the early days of the siege, late 1941.

2 One of the few routes into Leningrad was across Lake Ladoga, and this photograph shows horse-drawn sledges using the frozen waterway during the winter of 1941–42.

3 Soviet infantry advance under shell-fire to probe the encircling enemy forces around Leningrad, 1943.

4 German infantry man forward positions in wooded country around Leningrad, 1942.

5 Soviet infantry occupy a German trench close to Leningrad, January 1944.

6 A German shell explodes in a street in Leningrad.

The Wehrmacht
German forces in retreat

1 The commander of a PzKpfw VI Tiger prepares his next move during the traumatic retreat of 1944–45. The enclosed space of a battle tank is well portrayed; to the remainder of the crew this was their only view of the sky.

2 A PzKpfw V Panther advances cautiously through a village in Poland, August 1944; the Panther's high-velocity 7·5cm gun was one of the most effective anti-armour weapons to see service in World War II. It is closely followed by an Sd Kfz 7/1 half-track, mounting quadruple 2cm anti-aircraft guns.

1

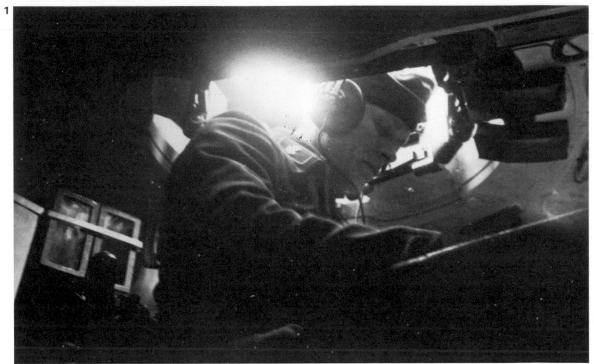

2

3 The reality of defeat: a dead German gunner lies amidst the shambles of his gun-pit in the aftermath of a Soviet attack. The weapon, broken and useless, is a 10·5cm *Leichte Feldhaubitze* LeFH 18. The photograph was probably taken in the vicinity of Minsk, July 1944.

4 A Panzer Grenadier, well kitted out in hooded combat smock, shelters beside a PzKpfw IV, Army Group South, May 1944. Note the *Schützen* armour and carefully positioned tree-trunk, both attempts to protect the tank against anti-armour weapons.

5 German infantry prepare to defend an elaborate trench position near Leningrad, July 1943. The machine gun is a 7·92mm *Maschinengewehr* MG42, introduced into Wehrmacht service in May 1942. It was a remarkable weapon, capable of an unprecedented rate of fire of 1200 rounds per minute, reliable and extremely resistant to the rigours of combat.

The Warsaw Uprising

1 Members of the Polish Home Army rush to occupy key points in Warsaw during the early hours of the uprising, 1 August 1944. At this time General Bor-Komorowski, the Polish commander, could muster a force of about 38,000 fighters actually in Warsaw, with a further 11,000 in the immediate vicinity, and when he pitted them against a German garrison of 40,000 initial success was achieved. By 5 August the Poles controlled about 60 per cent of the city and only isolated pockets of enemy forces remained.

2 Polish Home Army fighters, many in captured German helmets hastily painted with white recognition strips, occupy one of the telephone exchanges in Warsaw, early-August 1944. Although well-motivated and disciplined, the fighters were only lightly armed and once the Soviet offensive had ground to a halt on the other side of the Vistula, they were on their own against the German Army which used the full weight of modern armaments against the Home Army's position. After bitter fighting and large-scale destruction, Bor-Komorowski surrendered on 2 October.

3 Warsaw burns, 15 August 1944. Once the initial Polish attack had been absorbed in the first week of the uprising, the Germans slowly regained the initiative.

4 On the streets of Warsaw the Germans ordered their troops to conduct a 'scorched earth' response to the uprising. Here a group of soldiers manhandle a 7·5cm *Infanterie Kanone* 290 (r) – a weapon which started life as a Soviet Model 1927, only to be captured and taken into Wehrmacht service.

5/6 A remarkable pair of photographs, showing the arming and firing of a *Schwere Raketenwerfer* 61 battery in the streets of Warsaw, September 1944. The weapon consisted of a series of static frames into which were fitted 38cm *Sprenggranate* 4581 rockets.

5

6

Liberating the Balkans

1 Tanks of Panzer Division *Gross Deutschland* prepare to counterattack advancing Soviet forces, Iasy sector, Romania, May 1944. A row of battle-scarred PzKpfw IVs is on the left, with a PzKpfw VI Tiger on the right. The *Gross Deutschland* was the most favoured of the Army Panzer formations, receiving the best of the equipment available. As a result, however, it was always in the forefront of the fighting and spent the entire period of its divisional existence on the Eastern Front.

2 Soviet troops fire 82mm Model 1941 mortars in support of a local counter attack, Carpathian Mountains, October 1944. The Model 1941 was a unique weapon, transported as one piece with small stub axles at the lower end of the bipod legs onto which special wheels could be fitted, the whole thing being pulled along by a soldier.

3 Soviet infantry, armed with a DP 1928 light machine gun (left) and PPSh sub-machine gun, hold a commanding position in Budapest overlooking the Citadel, February 1945.

4 Don Cossack Guards move through a Romanian village, watched by the local inhabitants, August 1944.

5 Soviet infantry jump from the hulls of T-34s to engage enemy defensive positions, Budapest, late-December 1944. The Hungarian capital was encircled by 24 December but was not captured until the following February, after heavy fighting, especially around the Citadel.

6 Hungarian troops, dressed in uniforms similar to their German allies, prepare a defensive artillery position in the Carpathian foothills, September 1944. The Soviets attacked on 2 October, breaking through towards the Danube plain and causing the Hungarian Regent, Admiral Horthy, to attempt armistice negotiations. However, on Hitler's orders Horthy was deposed and bitter fighting ensued which was not to end until March 1945.

Chapter 8
Battle for the Pacific

1

1 Admiral William Halsey, one of the most successful US naval commanders of the Pacific War. Called in by Admiral Nimitz to conduct the naval campaign in the Solomons in 1942, Halsey was later responsible for the destruction of the Japanese carrier force at Leyte Gulf in October 1944.

2 General Sir William Slim, commander of the British Fourteenth Army in Burma, 1943–45. Slim was a tough but immensely popular leader whose campaign in the difficult terrain of Burma was one of the major successes of the war.

3 Major-General Claire L. Chennault (left), commander of the US Fourteenth Air Force in China, greets Major-General Albert Wedemeyer, newly appointed chief of staff to Chinese leader Chiang Kai-shek, late 1944.

4 Vice-Admiral Takeo Kurita, commander of the Japanese First Striking Force at the Battle of Leyte Gulf, October 1944.

5 Vice-Admiral Jisaburo Ozawa, commander of the Japanese Mobile (carrier) Fleet from November 1942 to the end of the war.

6 The battle of the Philippine Sea, June 1944

The counter-offensive against the Japanese in the Pacific began in the south, where success in Papua/New Guinea (Buna and Wau were retaken in January 1943) and victory on Guadalcanal (February 1943) gave the Allies under General MacArthur an initiative they fought hard to exploit. A two-pronged advance was planned – on the left in New Guinea and on the right in the Solomons – with the ultimate aim of seizing the Bismarck Archipelago and neutralising the Japanese base at Rabaul.

In New Guinea the campaign continued with the fall of Salamaua (12 September 1943), taken by a combination of Australian advances from Wau and American amphibious landings in Nassau Bay. The pattern was repeated to secure Lae four days later, after which the Allies struck north to encircle and capture the Huon Peninsula, an operation completed in April 1944. Three months later, after a series of amphibious landings along the northern coast of Hollandia, the whole of the island was in Allied hands.

By then the Solomons had been cleared. In June 1943 Rendova Island was seized, preparing the way for a successful campaign in New Georgia (21 June–25 August) during which Japanese naval power in the region was contained by sea battles such as Kula Gulf (5/6 July) and Vella Gulf (6 August) and by a sustained air offensive against ships and harbours. By late September New Zealand troops had cleared Vella Lavella, enabling American forces to capture Empress Augusta Bay (Bougainville) in November. US Marines landed at Cape Gloucester (western New Britain) on 26 December and two months later other American

units seized the Admiralty Islands to the north. Rabaul, encircled and heavily bombed, was left to 'wither on the vine', terminating a campaign which had seen some savage fighting.

Meanwhile, in the central Pacific Admiral Nimitz had also switched to the offensive, aiming to cut through the middle of the Japanese empire in an 'island-hopping' advance. After lengthy preparations, the offensive began on 13 November 1943 with air and naval bombardments of the Gilbert Islands. Amphibious landings took place a week later, encountering little resistance on the island of Makin but experiencing major problems on Tarawa, a triangular group of atolls and coral reefs, honeycombed with prepared defences. It was to take three days of particularly heavy fighting, during which the Americans lost nearly 1000 Marines, before Tarawa was secure. The same happened in February 1944, when the islands of Kwajalein and Eniwetok in the Marshalls were seized; it was apparent that the Japanese were prepared to fight fanatically to slow the American advance.

Nimitz rose to the challenge, choosing to project his forces a further 1600 km (1000 miles) westwards in June 1944 to attack Saipan in the Mariana Islands. Landings on 15 June were sharply contested, but of far more significance was the Japanese decision to commit naval forces to the battle. Early on 19 June the radars of Vice-Admiral Mitscher's Task Force 58 in the Philippine Sea spotted a wave of Japanese aircraft, launched from the carriers of Vice-Admiral Ozawa's First Mobile Fleet, heading for Saipan. In a series of furious air battles, later dubbed the 'Great Marianas Turkey Shoot' by victorious Ameri-

2

3

can pilots, over 300 Japanese planes were shot down and, in a submarine attack later in the day, two of Ozawa's carriers (*Taiho* and *Shokaku*) were sunk. A third (*Hiyo*) was destroyed by American aircraft on 20 June, forcing Ozawa to withdraw, having lost the battle of the Philippine Sea. The Americans were free to complete the capture of Saipan (9 July) and then to seize Guam and Tinian by 10 August.

Both Nimitz and MacArthur now turned towards the Philippines where, on 20 October 1944, landings were made on the east coast of Leyte Island. The Japanese, aware that this was a direct threat to their links with southern resource areas, responded by committing the whole of their Combined Fleet in a desperate effort to disrupt the assault. Ozawa's four remaining carriers (*Zuikaku, Zuiho, Chitose* and *Chiyoda*) moved towards Leyte Gulf from the north, aiming to divert American naval attention while other fleets attacked the landing force. But the operation was poorly co-ordinated and, in a series of separate engagements on 24/25 October – in the Sibuyan Sea, the Surigao Strait and off Samar Island – the Americans intercepted and destroyed the main attacking fleets. This enabled Admiral Halsey's US Third Fleet to concentrate against Ozawa and, in an action off Cape Engano (25/26 October) all four Japanese carriers were sunk. In desperation Japanese pilots mounted *kamikaze* (suicide) strikes, sinking the light carrier *St Lô*, but they could do little to alter the fact that the Americans had won the Battle of Leyte Gulf and gained undisputed naval supremacy. Leyte Island was cleared by 31 December.

The Japanese were under similar pressure in Burma. Since May 1942 the British had slowly gained experience in jungle warfare, partly through two abortive advances into Arakan (November 1942 and December 1943) and partly through the exploits of Brigadier Wingate's Chindits, who not only operated deep behind enemy lines (February–April 1943) but also aided General Stilwell's Sino-American forces as they thrust into northern Burma from China (October 1943–August 1944). Thus when the Japanese attacked Fourteenth Army positions on the Indian border in March 1944, the British held firm. Defensive locations at Imphal and Kohima were encircled, but General Slim refused to withdraw, supplying the garrisons by air and organising a counter-attack. Kohima was relieved on 18 April, and although Imphal was to continue under siege until 22 June, the heavy fighting destroyed Japanese strength. As they retreated, Slim followed, crossing the Chindwin River in late November and linking up with Sino-American units to complete the liberation of northern Burma on 15 December. By then, except in China (where a Japanese offensive in April 1944 had gained significant ground), the Allies stood poised to mount campaigns of victory throughout Southeast Asia and the Pacific.

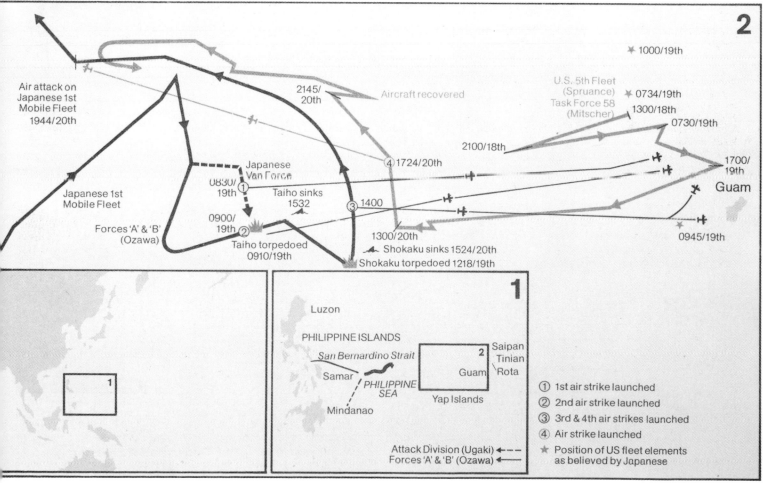

Tarawa

1 From the shelter of an improvised sandbag position, a US Marine throws grenades towards a Japanese bunker close to the airfield at Betio on the island of Tarawa, 21 November 1943. Although the coral outcrop of Betio was small, the Japanese deployed a garrison of 5000 men in carefully-prepared defensive locations. The preliminary air and naval bombardments (13–20 November) stunned the defenders enough to allow the Marines to get ashore on the 20th, but thereafter the Americans had to fight for every inch of ground.

2 Marine reinforcements come ashore at Betio, 22 November 1943, advancing up the beach past the litter of the initial assault wave. Poor communications and a lack of adequate landing vehicles delayed the commitment of American reserves, leaving the assault battalions to face the worst of the fighting alone. It was a lesson which was to be remembered.

3 Marines of the initial assault wave shelter behind a log barricade at the head of the invasion beach while others face the dangers of an exposed advance, Betio, 20/21 November 1943.

4 The aftermath of battle, Red Beach 3, Betio, showing the devastation caused by the fighting and the exposed nature of the landing area. On the right an Amtrac LVT (Landing Vehicle Tracked) lies derelict.

5 Prisoners are marched along a beach on Tarawa, 23 November 1943. Although the bulk of the Japanese garrison fought to the death, 17 wounded soldiers and 129 Korean labourers were taken prisoner.

6 Red Beach 2, Betio, in the aftermath of the battle, 23 November 1943. American losses on Tarawa – 984 dead and 2072 wounded – caused shocked concern in the United States at the time.

Retaking the Marianas

1 US Marines of the first assault wave take cover behind a sand-dune, Saipan, 15 June 1944. The Amtracs have brought the Marines right up to the shore-line, but the narrowness of the beach and lack of natural cover is delaying deployment. Nevertheless, within 20 minutes of the start of the attack, some 8000 Marines were ashore and, as warships pounded Japanese positions, eight small beach-heads were carved out. By nightfall 20,000 fighting troops had been landed, to face heavy resistance. The island was not secured until 9 July, by which time 27,000 Japanese and 3126 Americans had been killed.

2 'Water Buffalo' LVTs, armed with Browning machine guns fore and aft, carry Marines towards the shore at Tinian, 24 July 1944. Landings on two small beaches on the northeast coast of the island were successful, a Japanese counterattack on the night of 25/26 July was beaten off and the island secured by the 31st; 6050 Japanese and 290 Americans lost their lives. Tinian, together with the neighbouring islands of Saipan and Guam, were quickly transformed into elaborate air bases for B-29 bombers.

3 A battery of truck-mounted 4·5-inch M8 rockets fires at Japanese positions, Saipan, June 1944. Capable of carrying 2kg (4·2lb) of high explosive out to a range of 4200m (4600 yds), each M8 rocket could inflict significant damage, but the real value of the weapon was its impact when fired in salvo. In the Pacific campaign it proved particularly useful against Japanese bunkers.

4 Marines fire a lashed-down 105mm M3 howitzer point-blank at Japanese positions on Saipan, June 1944.

5 A Marine throws a grenade at a Japanese bunker, Saipan, June 1944. The difficult nature of the terrain, providing opportunities for effective defence, is well shown.

China
Japan's western front

1 Well-camouflaged Nationalist Chinese cross a stream in southern Yunnan, May 1944. When the Japanese occupied Burma in 1942, they came into contact with Chinese forces on the Salween River and threatened the supply route known as the Burma Road as it entered southeast China in Yunnan province.

2 Lieutenant General Sakai of the Imperial Japanese Army rides in triumph through Hong Kong, late-December 1941. The loss of Hong Kong was a humiliating defeat for Britain, but until the Japanese had been defeated in mainland China, there was little that could be done to reverse the situation. In the event, Hong Kong was not liberated until after the Japanese surrender in 1945.

3 US Air Force personnel talk with a Chinese pilot as Curtiss Hawk fighters are prepared for operations against the Japanese. The air threat to China had been considerable at the time of the Japanese invasion in 1937 and Chiang Kai-shek, the Nationalist leader, relied upon American aid.

4 A Japanese soldier stands guard as supplies are moved by train somewhere in China. The need to secure lines of communication in an area as vast as China tied down substantial Japanese forces throughout the war.

5 Well-equipped Chinese infantry celebrate a local victory over the Japanese, Hunan province, May 1945. Once the Allies had regained the initiative in the Pacific and Southeast Asia, the Chinese were able to mount telling offensives against stretched and demoralised enemy forces.

6 Chinese gunners fire an American-supplied M3 howitzer during the drive towards Kweilin, capital of Kwangsi province, July 1945. Chiang Kai-shek's forces were heavily dependent upon American supplies throughout the Sino-Chinese War.

The forgotten army
British troops in Burma

1 Colonel Michael Calvert (with arm outstretched), commander of the 77th (Long Range Penetration) Brigade, briefs Major Freddie Shaw, while another Chindit looks on, during the battle for Mogaung, the culmination of the Second Chindit Operation, June 1944. Faced by a relentless enemy and isolated inside a highly inhospitable terrain many British soldiers in Burma considered themselves to be a 'forgotten army'. In addition, a series of tactical reverses suffered at Japanese hands throughout 1942 and 1943 further undermined morale, but Chindit operations – conducted deep behind Japanese lines – helped restore confidence and dispel the myth of Japanese invincibility.

2 Gurkhas of the 7th Indian Division advance past Japanese dead during the fighting around the Ngakyedauk Pass, Arakan, February 1944. The second Arakan operation had begun in December 1943 but Japanese counter-attacks around Ngakyedauk halted the advance and encircled two Indian divisions. Sustained by air re-supply, they held off the Japanese and inflicted the first major land defeat on the Japanese in Burma.

3 A Japanese Type 97 medium tank, well-camouflaged against air attack, crosses open country in northwestern Burma, May 1942. The Type 97 was an up-gunned version of the Type 95, fielding a 57mm main armament, but it proved no match for the British M4 Shermans encountered later in the campaign.

4 A Chindit patrol advances north from Indaw along a jungle track during the Second Chindit Operation, April 1944. The use of mules as pack animals was crucial to the mobility of the LRP columns; these animals are laden with mortar bombs and ammunition boxes.

1

2

5 Supply canisters are para-dropped from a C47 Dakota of No. 1 Air Commando Group onto a pre-selected jungle clearing, Second Chindit Operation, 1944. The use of air re-supply was central to Wingate's LRP scheme and the task was carried out effectively by the specially-formed No. 1 Air Commando Group, commanded by US Colonel Philip E. Cochran.

6 A Japanese answer to the problem of difficult terrain in the Far East was to issue their troops with bicycles. Here an infantry soldier, his machine well-laden with supplies and kit, negotiates a log bridge over a Burmese stream in 1942.

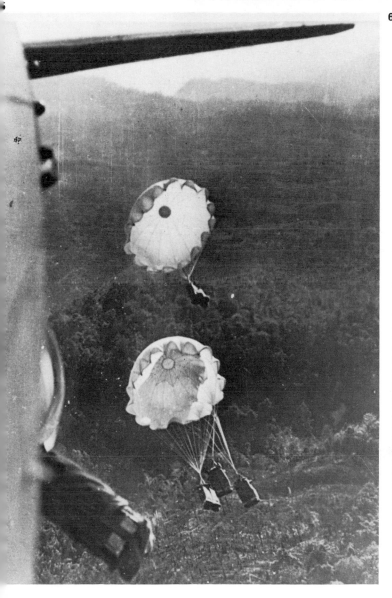

Leyte Gulf
The death throes of the Japanese Navy

1 The Japanese battleship *Yamato* at sea, 1944. Designed to outclass all other battleships in the world, she was an impressive fighting platform, weighing in at 71,000 tons and mounting nine 460mm (18·1-inch) guns as her main armament. Unfortunately the *Yamato* and her sister-ship the *Musashi* were obsolete by the time of their commitment to the Pacific War; the battleship was no longer supreme in an age of the aircraft carrier. Both ships took part in the Battle of Leyte Gulf in October 1944, during which the *Musashi* was sunk and the *Yamato* badly damaged.

2 The Japanese carrier *Zuiho* comes under air attack during the engagement off Cape Engano, 25 October 1944. One of four carriers under Vice-Admiral Ozawa which were meant to act as a decoy fleet, drawing American naval units away from protecting the Leyte landings, *Zuiho* was hit and destroyed by aircraft from the American carrier *Enterprise*. The elaborate camouflage patterns to be seen on this photograph were Japanese attempts to break up the shape of the carrier when viewed from the air.

3 The battleship *Yamato* under air attack in the Sibuyan Sea, 24 October 1944. Although hit by several bombs (one of which may be seen exploding close to the aft turret), the battleship survived Leyte Gulf, only to be sacrificed in a desperate attempt to disrupt the Okinawa landings in April 1945. Given enough fuel for a one-way trip, the *Yamato* was intercepted and sunk by aircraft from nine American carriers en route. Her loss, and that of *Musashi* in the Sibuyan Sea on 24 October 1944, symbolised the new era of naval warfare.

4 Part of the huge US invasion fleet prepares for the attack on Leyte Island, October 1944. It was this force which the Japanese hoped to disperse and destroy in their naval attacks on Leyte Gulf.

5 With anti-aircraft guns blazing, the escort carrier USS *Sangamon* reacts to Japanese air attacks, Leyte, November 1944. Grumman F6F Hellcats – the most effective American carrier-borne fighters of World War II – stand on deck. Hellcats accounted for 4947 of the 6477 enemy aircraft destroyed in the air by US Navy carrier pilots.

Chapter 9
The Italian campaign

1

1 General Mark W. Clark, commander of the US Fifth Army at the time of the Salerno landings, September 1943. He led his forces through the difficult drive north in 1943–44, organising the Anzio landings (January 1944) and liberating Rome (June 1944). Given command of 15th Army Group in December 1944, Clark continued to conduct Allied operations until the German surrender in Italy in May 1945.

2 Field Marshal Albert Kesselring, commander of German forces in Italy, waves his baton in salute as he leaves a paratroop headquarters near Cassino, April 1944. He is sitting in the back of an NSU HK101, half-tracked motorcycle.

3 South African troops of the Kimberley Regiment (Imperial Light Horse), 6th South African Armoured Division, enter Florence aboard Universal Carriers, 4 August 1944, accompanied by anti-fascist partisans. Part of the British XIII Corps, the 6th Armoured had arrived in Italy in May 1944 – in time for the final Cassino battles – and was to see hard fighting from the Gothic Line to the Po Valley before the war was over.

By mid-1943, with victory in North Africa and air and naval supremacy in the Mediterranean, the Allies were free to open up a new front in southern Europe. They concentrated against the Italians and after a three-week aerial bombardment, the fortress island of Pantellaria, mid-way between Tunis and Sicily, was seized (11 June). A month later (10 July), General Alexander's 15th Army Group invaded Sicily itself in Operation 'Husky'. General Patton's US Seventh Army landed on the Allied left, in the Gulf of Gela, while General Montgomery's British Eighth Army assaulted on the right, in the Gulf of Syracuse. Airborne landings, designed to secure beach exits, were disrupted by poor weather, but a German counter-attack of 11/12 July failed, enabling the Allies to push northwards. When Montgomery met stiff resistance at Catania (18 July), Patton immediately swung east to take the enemy in the rear while simultaneously despatching forces to clear the west of the island. The capture of Messina, in the extreme north east, marked the end of the campaign (17 August).

Italian public opinion turned against the fascist regime: Mussolini was overthrown on 24 July and his successors approached the Allies to discuss peace terms. An armistice was signed on 3 September as Eighth Army units crossed the Straits of Messina to land in Calabria (Operation 'Baytown'), although the details were not made public until the 8th when, it was hoped, Allied forces would be in position to occupy all of southern Italy. But the Germans, realising the danger, sent reinforcements under Field-Marshal Kesselring to the Naples area and when the main Allied landings took place on 9 September at Salerno (Operation 'Avalanche'), the enemy was waiting. A simultaneous British landing at Taranto (Operation 'Slapstick') failed to divert German attention, leaving the Salerno forces – General Mark Clark's Fifth Army, comprising one British and one American corps – to face tough opposition. It was only after reinforcements had been rushed ashore that the Germans were pushed back, with Clark and Montgomery linking up on 16 September.

Kesselring withdrew to the Gustav Line, a series of prepared defences along the Garigliano and Sangro Rivers to the north of Naples, where rugged terrain and deteriorating weather stalled the Allied advance. An attempt by the Fifth Army to push across the flooded Volturno River in the west on 12 October ground to a halt and the Eighth Army, by now responsible for the eastern sector, fared no better later in the month. On 15 November Alexander halted all operations. It was a low point for the Allies – elsewhere in the Mediterranean a British

attempt to seize the Dodecanese Islands between Greece and Turkey, initiated on 10 September, was abandoned on 16 November – and as winter set in, further drives against the Gustav Line met with failure. In late November the Fifth Army bogged down in front of the Rapido River, and although the Eighth Army made some progress in the east, capturing Ortona on 27 December, the main German defences, particularly around the key town of Cassino in the centre of Clark's sector, held out.

The Allies tried to by-pass the problem. On 22 January 1944 the US VI Corps under Major-General Lucas landed at Anzio to the north of the Gustav Line in Operation 'Shingle', catching the enemy by surprise. Although beach-heads were easily secured, an advance inland was delayed, and the Germans organised a counter-attack (16–19 February) which very nearly succeeded. Lucas was replaced on 23 February, but by then it was too late; Anzio degenerated into a siege, leaving Clark with little alternative beyond frontal assaults in the

2

3

4 Benito Mussolini (wearing a side-cap), accompanied by Italian and German officers, inspects the pro-fascist *Monterosa* Division, 17 July 1944. By this time Mussolini was little more than a figure-head.

5 Cassino, Anzio and the drive to Rome.

Cassino area. In fact initial operations had been carried out in January to coincide with the Anzio landings, but had been extremely costly. Further attacks in February – during which the historic Benedictine monastery atop Monte Cassino was destroyed by Allied bombing (15 February) – were no more successful, and Alexander, as overall commander, was forced to regroup. A new offensive began on 11 May, in better weather, with the intention of taking Cassino in a pincer move. The fighting was extremely hard, but both the Rapido and Garigliano were crossed and, on 18 May, Polish troops finally captured the monastery ruins. Almost immediately the forces at Anzio launched a breakout operation; by 25 May they had linked up with the rest of the Fifth Army. The Gustav Line fell apart, opening the road to Rome, which fell on 4 June.

But the campaign was not over. As Allied forces exploited their success by driving north, the Germans once more made use of the mountain chains. Although the unfinished Albert and Arno Lines were easily overrun and the potentially formidable Gothic Line was breached in both west and east, the Allies soon experienced familiar problems. The Eighth Army had to fight hard to control the Gemmano and Coriano Ridges to the south of Rimini, while the Fifth Army failed to take Bologna; by late October the weather had broken and the Allies had dug in. Some progress was made in the east towards the Senio River during the ensuing winter, but to all intents and purposes the Italian campaign had, once again, ground to a halt.

A new Allied offensive began on 9 April 1945 with attacks towards Ferrara in the east. The Germans were caught off-balance, particularly by an amphibious operation across Lake Comacchio, and when the Fifth Army joined in five days later, enemy defences collapsed. As Alexander's forces swept into the Po Valley and advanced to link up with Allied units driving south from France and Austria, a surrender was negotiated, which came into effect on 2 May.

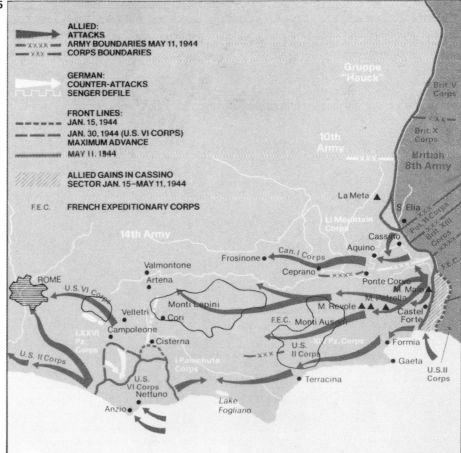

ALLIED:
ATTACKS
ARMY BOUNDARIES MAY 11, 1944
CORPS BOUNDARIES

GERMAN:
COUNTER-ATTACKS
SENGER DEFILE

FRONT LINES:
JAN. 15, 1944
JAN. 30, 1944 (U.S. VI CORPS)
MAXIMUM ADVANCE
MAY 11, 1944

ALLIED GAINS IN CASSINO
SECTOR JAN. 15–MAY 11, 1944

F.E.C. FRENCH EXPEDITIONARY CORPS

Invasion of Sicily

1 German troops hold out a flag for aerial recognition, Sicily, July, 1943. The Luftwaffe was still strong enough to provide some air support to the forces on the ground.

2 British gunners fire a 6-pounder, 7 cwt anti-tank gun at an already-battered SdKfz 251 half-track, Sicily, July 1943. The 6-pounder had been developed in 1938 but production was delayed and it was not until September 1941 that the Royal Artillery first took the weapon into action. The 6-pounder was a considerable improvement over its predecessor, the 2-pounder, and saw service throughout the war.

3 American troops advance warily through an isolated clump of trees. Note the white strip on the back of the helmets and 'Stars and Stripes' armbands, worn for recognition purposes.

4 British infantry push through the outskirts of a burning village during the fighting around Catania, 18 July 1943. The man in the lead carries a Thompson sub-machine gun, while the other two members of the patrol are armed with ·303-inch Lee-Enfield rifles.

5 Allied co-operation on Sicily – a British brigadier talks to American troops, possibly at Messina, August 1943. On the surface, co-operation between the Allies was good, but in reality the personality clash between Patton and Montgomery, epitomised by the 'race to Messina' (which Patton won by a matter of hours), augured ill for the future.

6 British troops wade ashore from an American landing ship, Gulf of Syracuse, 10 July 1943.

Salerno
The Allies invade Italy

1 The crew of a British wire-laying jeep take cover as a shell explodes perilously close to their vehicle, Reggio di Calabria, September 1943. The jeep – or, to give it the official American designation, the 'Truck, ¼ ton, 4 × 4, Command Reconnaissance' vehicle – was a Willys design of 1940 which appeared in many guises throughout the Allied armed forces.

2 German troops set up an 8.1cm *Granatwerfer* 34 mortar, Salerno area, September 1943. The GrW 34 was the standard German infantry mortar of World War II, two examples being held by each rifle company.

3 An American infantryman in action with his Thompson sub-machine gun. The unexpected nature of the German opposition around the landing beaches at Salerno led to hard fighting.

4 A British military policeman (left) directs a Universal (or 'Bren-Gun') Carrier ashore from an LCT (landing craft, tank), Salerno, September 1943. Bedford 4 × 2 three-ton trucks – the mainstay of the British logistics effort in all theatres – stand on the right.

5 A *Sturmgeschutz* (StuG) III, Ausf G in action, southern Italy, September 1943. Based upon the chassis of the PzKpfw III, Ausf J, this model of the StuG III, armed with the long 7·5cm *Sturmkanone* 40, first appeared in late 1942. Armour skirting, designed to protect the wheels and tracks from attack, was common fit by 1943 – indication of more effective Allied anti-tank capability.

6 British troops advance through a vineyard in southern Italy, September 1943. The advantages of khaki may be appreciated as the men blend easily into the light and shade of the surrounding bushes. All are wearing the standard 1937-Pattern infantry webbing and equipment and, as the empty scabbards show, are advancing with bayonets fixed.

Monte Cassino
Germany's mountain stronghold

1 German troops, including at least one parachutist, shelter in the ruins of a house in Cassino town, Spring 1944. Their StuG III Ausf G, with long 7·5cm gun, has been parked alongside, ready to fire from its concealed position, and a rack of *Steilhandgranaten* 39 'stick grenades' is available for instant use.

2 A German paratrooper in a carefully-prepared defensive position stands guard with his 7·92mm MG42 machine gun.

3 Cassino town under bombardment, early 1944. Castle Hill may be seen, top right, and the mountainous nature of the terrain appreciated.

4 The moment of victory: the Polish flag is raised amid the ruins of Cassino monastery, 18 May 1944.

5 British troops engaged in the difficult and dangerous task of house-clearance, Cassino area, early 1944. As one soldier covers the doorway, his colleague kicks his way in.

6 The mud of Italy was a perpetual problem, made worse by the unexpectedly wet summers of 1943 and 1944. Here a British gunner works hard to free a 5·5 inch gun-howitzer.

Anzio and the drive to Rome

1 A British M4 Sherman comes ashore from an LCT (landing craft, tank), Anzio, 22 January 1944. The unopposed nature of the landing is apparent, although both LCT and tank have ·50-inch Browning machine guns fitted for anti-aircraft defence. Despite landing some 50,000 troops during the first 48 hours, the Anzio assault was a failure as the Allied commander, Major-General John Lucas, did not push his forces inland to take the surrounding high ground.

2 Pipers of Scottish regiments march through the streets of Rome, June 1944. Only a few weeks earlier Allied troops taken at Anzio had been paraded along the same stretch of road by their German captors.

3 American troops advance through the town of Nettuno, January 1944, adopting the usual formation for advance in a built-up area.

4 German armour, Anzio, early 1944. On the right is a PzKpfw VI Tiger; in the centre, travelling away from the camera, is a PzKpfw IV, heavily laden with spare road-wheels; on the left, partially obscured by bushes, is an SdKfz 251 half-track. The vehicles belong to the *Hermann Goering* Panzer Division, part of which fought at Anzio.

5 German paratroops mount their BMW R750 motor-cycle combinations, outskirts of Rome, June 1944. The R750 was a heavy machine – it weighed 400kg (882lb) in its basic form – but proved to be mobile and robust under combat conditions. Designed to carry two or (as here) three fully-armed soldiers, it could cover rough terrain and maintain a high cruising speed.

6 American troops, mounted on the ubiquitous jeep, enter Rome, 4 June 1944. The crowd seems unsure of its welcome, although the presence of a British soldier implies that these were not the first Allied troops to pass by.

Advance to the Alps
The final battles in Italy

1 American troops, suitably kitted out, in northern Italy, winter 1944–45. The man on the left is carrying a Springfield Model 1903A4 sniper rifle (with Weaver 330C telescopic sights); the one in the centre has an ordinary issue M1 Garand and his colleague on the right a Thompson sub-machine gun. The M1903 Springfield, as its numerical designation suggests, was an old bolt-action rifle which saw service during World War I; most examples were withdrawn during the early months of World War II.

2 German prisoners march under British guard into captivity, northern Italy, April 1945. The officer on the left in the front rank is a member of the Mountain Troops.

3 A British 3·7 inch Mark VI heavy anti-aircraft gun being fired in the ground-support role, northern Italy, April 1945. It took some time for the British to copy the German idea of using anti-aircraft guns against ground targets, but when they did, the 3·7 inch proved a useful weapon. The Mark VI was heavy – it weighed over 20 tonnes – but could fire a 12·7kg (28lb) shell to the quite extraordinary distance of 41,148m (45,000 yds).

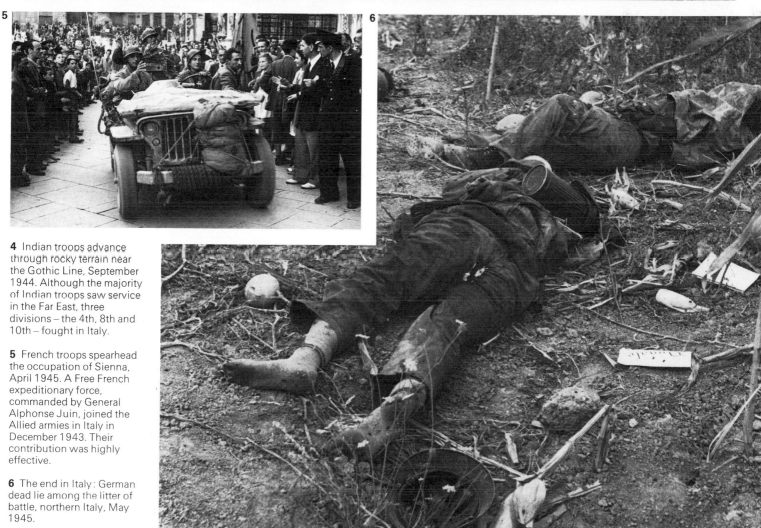

4 Indian troops advance through rocky terrain near the Gothic Line, September 1944. Although the majority of Indian troops saw service in the Far East, three divisions – the 4th, 8th and 10th – fought in Italy.

5 French troops spearhead the occupation of Sienna, April 1945. A Free French expeditionary force, commanded by General Alphonse Juin, joined the Allied armies in Italy in December 1943. Their contribution was highly effective.

6 The end in Italy: German dead lie among the litter of battle, northern Italy, May 1945.

Chapter 10
Invasion of Europe

1 Field Marshal Gerd von Runstedt (left), German C-in-C West, greets Colonel General Heinz Guderian at his HQ in France, mid-1944. Von Runstedt was relieved of his command in July 1944 in the face of Allied success in Normandy, and although he was reappointed C-in-C West in September he was dismissed again in March 1945.

2 The Allied land commanders in Normandy, July 1944. From left to right: General George S. Patton Jr, commander of the newly-arrived US Third Army; General Omar Bradley, commander of the US First Army; General Sir Bernard Montgomery, commander of the Anglo-Canadian Second Army. When Eisenhower arrived to take overall command on 1 September 1944, Bradley assumed responsibility for 12th Army Group and Montgomery for 21st Army Group.

3 The Allied command team for D-Day, June 1944. From left to right: Admiral Sir Bertram Ramsay, naval commander; General Dwight D. Eisenhower, supreme commander; Air Chief Marshal Sir Arthur Tedder, deputy supreme commander; General Sir Bernard Montgomery, overall land commander during the initial stages of the invasion.

There had been calls for a 'Second Front', for an invasion of German-occupied Europe, since 1942, and plans for an Anglo-American invasion – Operation 'Overlord' – were drafted in Washington in May 1943. By then, however, the Germans had enjoyed three years in which to prepare the defences of the 'Atlantic Wall', and although they had proved vulnerable to surprise commando raids such as Bruneval (27/28 February 1942) and St Nazaire (28 March 1942), they were confident in their ability to withstand a large-scale amphibious assault, particularly since the disastrous Canadian landing at Dieppe on 19 August 1942. Allied preparations for 'Overlord' had therefore to be meticulous. The heavily defended Pas de Calais area was avoided and the less obvious beaches of Normandy earmarked for assault; a campaign of aerial interdiction, designed to disrupt enemy defences throughout northern France, was initiated on 1 April 1944; an elaborate deception plan was put into effect to divert German attention away from Normandy; a massive build-up of men and supplies took place in Britain; and a simultaneous invasion of southern France (Operation 'Anvil') was planned. 'D-Day' for the Normandy landings was set for 5 June 1944, although poor weather forced the Supreme Commander, General Eisenhower, to impose a 24-hour delay at the last moment.

The invasion began at 0200 hours on 6 June, when American and British airborne divisions landed respectively on the western and eastern flanks of the assault area. Some of the drops were hopelessly scattered, but others were accurate enough for key bridges and reinforcement choke-points to be captured or destroyed; an operation enhanced by concurrent French Resistance activity and continued interdiction bombing. At 0314 aircraft began to attack beach defences and at 0550 naval gunfire from an enormous invasion fleet offshore added to the weight of preliminary bombardment. Forty minutes later the first landing craft approached the shore, carrying men of General Bradley's US First Army, responsible for 'Utah' and 'Omaha' beaches in the west, and General Montgomery's Anglo-Canadian Second Army, aiming for 'Sword', 'Juno' and 'Gold' in the east. With the exception of 'Omaha', where rough seas and unexpectedly-stiff resistance caused problems, the Allies – aided by specially adapted armoured vehicles – quickly established viable beach-heads, linked up with pockets of airborne troops, fought off local counter-attacks from units of Rommel's Army Group B and set up special artificial harbours ('Mulberries') through which supplies and reinforcements began to pass.

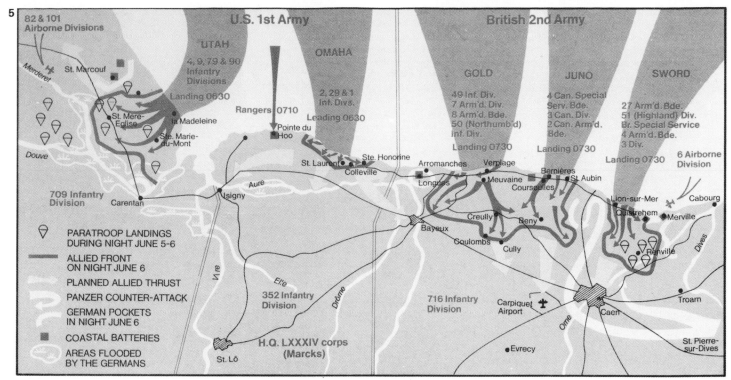

82 & 101
Airborne Divisions

U.S. 1st Army

British 2nd Army

UTAH

4, 9, 79 & 90
Infantry
Divisions
Landing 0630

OMAHA

Rangers 0710

2, 29 & 1
Inf. Divs.
Leading 0630

GOLD

49 Inf. Div.
7 Arm'd. Div.
8 Arm'd. Bde.
50 (Northumb'd)
Inf. Div.
Landing 0730

JUNO

4 Can. Special
Serv. Bde.
3 Can. Div.
2 Can. Arm'd.
Bde.
Landing 0730

SWORD

27 Arm'd. Bde.
51 (Highland) Div.
Br. Special Service
4 Arm'd. Bde.
3 Div.
Landing 0730

6 Airborne
Division

709 Infantry
Division

352 Infantry
Division

716 Infantry
Division

Carpiquet
Airport

H.Q. LXXXIV corps
(Marcks)

PARATROOP LANDINGS
DURING NIGHT JUNE 5-6

ALLIED FRONT
ON NIGHT JUNE 6

PLANNED ALLIED THRUST

PANZER COUNTER-ATTACK

GERMAN POCKETS
IN NIGHT JUNE 6

COASTAL BATTERIES

AREAS FLOODED
BY THE GERMANS

4 General Charles de
Gaulle, leader of the Free
French forces and future
president of France, June
1944. The position of de
Gaulle as an Allied leader
who, before August 1944,
did not hold political power
in the country he
represented, had led to him
being virtually ignored in the
planning for D-Day. He was
not to forgive the Anglo-
Americans easily.

5 The Allied landings on
D-Day.

Montgomery, acting as overall land commander during the assault phase, soon discovered that the main weight of enemy opposition was concentrated around Caen, preventing an Anglo-Canadian advance but leaving the Americans in the west relatively free to manoeuvre. By 17 June Bradley's troops had cut across the Cotentin peninsula to the Atlantic coast, and ten days later they liberated Cherbourg, although not before the Germans had destroyed the port facilities. Meanwhile, Montgomery had conducted a deliberate policy of attrition around Caen, designed to wear down enemy units. It proved to be a costly business – Operation 'Epsom' (26–30 June) achieved little, while Operation 'Goodwood' (18–20 July) only managed to capture Caen after heavy losses and bitter fighting – but German reserve formations (released piecemeal as Hitler still believed that an Allied attack on the Pas de Calais was imminent) were drawn in and significantly weakened. As a result, they were not available to oppose an American drive south from St Lô on 25 July (Operation 'Cobra'). Avranches fell on 1 August, after which General Patton's newly arrived Third Army poured westwards into Brittany and swung eastwards to take the forces still around Caen in the rear. As the encirclement developed, the German Fifth Panzer and Seventh Armies abandoned their equipment and withdrew eastwards through the Falaise-Argentan gap, harried by Allied fighter-bombers.

The German position was further undermined on 15 August when the invasion of southern France, delayed by a shortage of landing craft and now code-named 'Dragoon', finally took place. Spearheaded by General Patch's US Seventh Army, Allied forces established beach-heads between Toulon and Cannes against light opposition, after which General de Lattre de Tassigny's French II Corps pushed inland, liberating Toulon

and Marseilles and trapping the German Nineteenth Army around Montélimar. By 29 August the Allies were advancing rapidly up the Rhône Valley, linking up with Patton's forces on 11 September. Thereafter, as 6th Army Group under General Devers, they turned east to advance in line with the units from Normandy. By then the latter had liberated Paris (25 August), Eisenhower had arrived in Europe to assume overall command (1 September) and Montgomery and Bradley – now commanding 21st and 12th Army Groups respectively – had swept into Belgium and Luxembourg.

It was at this point, however, that a major strategic disagreement occurred within the Allied camp. Montgomery and Bradley favoured a single thrust towards the industrial area of the Ruhr, only to be overruled by Eisenhower who, conscious of acute supply problems (everything had still to be transported all the way from the Normandy beaches) and fearful of German counter-attacks, insisted on a broad-front advance, at least as far as the Rhine. Montgomery may have been trying to prove his point when, in early September, he suggested Operation 'Market Garden', an ambitious plan whereby American and British airborne troops would be dropped ahead of 21st Army Group to seize bridges over the myriad of waterways which threatened to delay an advance into Holland. The attack was launched on 17 September and enjoyed some initial success – by the 20th British armoured units had linked up with American paras and captured bridges at Veghel, Grave and Nijmegen – but stiffening German resistance prevented a breakthrough to relieve the British 1st Airborne Division at Arnhem. By 26 September the operation had been abandoned for the loss of nearly 7000 British paras and Montgomery's single-thrust ideal was discredited.

Dieppe
A hard-fought lesson

1

2

1 Assault boats, one of them discharging smoke to cover their approach, race for the landing beaches, Dieppe, 19 August 1942. Despite their speed and low silhouette, these boats show how far the Allies still had to go in the development of specialised landing craft for amphibious operations. Each could carry only a small number of men and, at Dieppe, there not enough of them to ensure constant support for the troops once they were ashore.

2 The scene on the landing beach at the end of the Dieppe operation: an LCT burns while Churchill tanks (all belonging to the Canadian 14th Tank Battalion) lie disabled on the beach.

3

4

3 A knocked-out Churchill rests on White Beach with the Casino in the background. The close proximity of buildings – each one of which could (and often did) conceal a German defensive position – was a major error in the Dieppe plan but a lesson well learnt for the future: on D-Day in June 1944 all five beaches were situated away from major towns.

4 Canadian dead lie where they fell, among the wire defences at the sea wall in front of Dieppe. Major-General Roberts' 2nd Canadian Division lost over 900 men killed (18 per cent of its total strength of 5000) plus many more captured in a single day's fighting.

5 British commandos, with an American Ranger NCO, return to Newhaven at the end of the Dieppe operation, 19 August 1942. Few Americans took part in the raid and those that did joined 'A' Commando, Royal Marines, committed to the desperate fight on White Beach at about 0830 hours. After heavy fighting they were withdrawn. Elsewhere, commandos had mixed fortunes – No 4 Commando, on the right flank, achieved their objectives but No 3 Commando on the left experienced real problems – and a total of 247 out of 1057 failed to return.

6 Canadian prisoners at Dieppe, guarded by members of the German 302nd Infantry Division. The Canadians lost over 2000 men as prisoners of war: their 2nd Division virtually ceased to exist after the operation.

The D-Day landings

1 British commandos wade ashore from their LCI (landing craft, infantry) while LCTs disgorge second echelon supplies, including prefabricated trackways, Gold Beach, 6 June 1944. The development of specialised landing vessels was one of the essential prerequisites of success and is indicative of the scale of Allied preparations.

2 American troops follow their officer ashore at the Normandy beaches, 6 June 1944. Other troops may be seen in the background, fanning out into the rather exposed coastal hinterland, while DUKWs (amphibious 6 × 6 wheeled transport vehicles) and M3 half-tracks towing 57mm anti-tank guns hug the shoreline.

3 GIs watch as German prisoners carry a wounded colleague towards a POW assembly area on the Normandy beaches.

4 Darkness descends on the night of 6 June and barrage balloons are deployed to protect the invasion fleet. LSTs continue to offload men and supplies onto one of the American beaches. Altogether on 6 June some 4000 ships carried 176,000 troops and their supplies to the lodgment area.

5 Not all the Allied troops made it ashore easily: here an American soldier is dragged out of the water half-drowned after the LCI in which he was travelling had been knocked out.

6 The airborne landings of 5/6 June were an integral part of Operation Overlord, securing vital rear areas prior to the seaborne landings. The price was high, however, as these dead Americans testify.

Caen
Stalemate and slaughter

1 An ammunition truck hit by artillery fire explodes spectacularly on a road to the east of Caen, July 1944.

2 British infantry shelter behind an earth bank as the advance out of the Orne River salient grinds to a halt, Operation Goodwood, 18 July 1944. Despite massive artillery and air bombardments, German defensive positions were still largely intact when the Goodwood attack began.

3 Shermans of a British armoured unit push forward in lightly wooded country towards Caumont, July 1944. The extra tracks positioned on the front glacis are for added protection.

4 Hawker Typhoon IB fighter-bombers (with 'bubble' canopies) on a forward airstrip in Normandy, July 1944. All seem to be fitted with the underwing rockets – four each side – that were to cause such devastation to German vehicles.

5 The British 34,000-ton battleship HMS *Rodney* provides long-range support for troops on shore, Normandy, June 1944. The provision of such a heavy weight of fire – *Rodney* was equipped with nine 16-inch, twelve 6-inch and six 4·7-inch guns – was a definite advantage to the Allies throughout the summer.

6 British Churchill tanks are guided across a prefabricated 'scissors' bridge, Dives River area, east of Falaise, August 1944. The Churchill was developed as an infantry-support tank but by the time it entered service in 1942 such designations had ceased to have any meaning.

7 Engineers of the Canadian 2nd Division approach the town of Falaise from the north, sweeping the ground for mines.

8 A 5·5-inch medium artillery piece lays down supporting fire, Operation Totalize, Falaise, August 1944.

FALAISE

139

Germany's counter-attack

1 PzKpfw VI Ausf E Tiger Is of the *schwere* (heavy) SS Panzer Abteilung 101, 1st SS Panzer Corps, advance en route to Normandy. On 12 June these same tanks, commanded by SS *Hauptsturmführer* Michael Wittmann, ambushed and virtually annihilated the 4th County of London Yeomanry.

2 A German soldier tends British wounded in the aftermath of the abortive attacks around Caen, Operation Epsom, late-June 1944.

3/4 German infantry, well-equipped with machine guns and ammunition, move up to oppose the Allied drive across the Odon River, late-June 1944.

5 With the names of girl-friends adorning cupola and driver's viewing-port, the youthful crew of a PzKpfw IV of 12th SS Panzer Division *Hitler-Jugend* prepare to advance to the west of Caen, June 1944. The tank has been covered with *Zimmerit* anti-magnetic paste.

6 A well-camouflaged 5cm Pak 38 anti-tank gun in an ambush position awaits the arrival of Allied armour on the outskirts of Caen, June 1944.

7 German troops prepare a 15cm *Nebelwerfer* 41 rocket launcher in wooded country around Caen, in summer 1944. The *Nebelwerfer*, known to the Allies as 'Moaning Minnie', first appeared in 1942 and the six barrels were mounted on a two-wheeled carriage with a split trail.

Normandy
The American breakout

1 The crew of an American M8 armoured car view the results of artillery fire on houses in the French village of Canisy, to the southwest of St Lô, attacked by Combat Command A, 2nd Armored Division, on 25 July 1944 in the early stages of Operation Cobra. The M8 has its turret, mounting the 37mm gun, reversed.

2 A PzKpfw V Panther of SS Panzer Regiment 2, 2nd SS Panzer Division *Das Reich*, lies abandoned on the Coutances-St Lô road as American armour (an M31 armoured recovery vehicle is shown in the foreground) thunders past, 28 July 1944. The *Das Reich* Division had only recently arrived in Normandy after a traumatic move from Toulouse during which it had come under constant attack from French Resistance fighters. Elements of the division had retaliated with massacres of civilians at Tulle, Oradour-sur-Glane and Mussidan (9–11 June). SS Panzer Regiment 2 was to see hard fighting from St Lô to the Falaise pocket, losing nearly all its tanks in the process.

3 American infantry fire on enemy positions from the shelter of a typical *bocage* bank, Operation Cobra, late-July 1944. The *bocage* proved a nightmare for the Allies, comprising a seemingly endless series of fields surrounded by high earthen banks, many with close hedging on top. The soldier on the left has just fired an M17 rifle grenade.

4 American infantry crouch low as they cross a road near St Lô, late-July 1944. The remains of a German column – comprising transport vehicles and, close to the camera, a PzKpfw V Panther – litter the carriageway.

5 Sherman tanks move warily towards Avranches, their 75mm guns covering both sides of the road, 29 July 1944. The wrecked vehicles on the right are probably German transport carts, destroyed by Allied air power. the dead horses were a constant and long-remembered feature of the Normandy campaign.

6 A fallen tree and part of a ruined building provide cover for American infantrymen as their colleagues race down the main street of the apparently deserted village of St Ensy in Normandy, July 1944. As each house could contain a German sniper or machine-gun nest, such advances had to be treated with care.

4

5

6

Anvil and Dragoon
The invasion of southern France

1 An American M10 tank destroyer, its turret reversed, moves through a French town to the north of Montélimar, 4 September 1944, passing the remains of a German column hit by air and artillery fire. The M10, developed in 1942, comprised a 3-inch (76·2mm) gun built on an adapted M4 Sherman chassis with an open-topped turret and flat-topped hull. Its primary role was, as its name implies, to take on enemy tanks.

2 A French sailor (probably a member of the FFI – French Forces of the Interior), inspects the workings of an abandoned German 5cm Pak 38 anti-tank gun, sited to command one of the main streets in Marseilles, late-August 1944. The city was liberated on 28 August.

3 A column of M8 howitzer motor carriages of the French 1st Armoured Division advances into Marseilles, 28 August 1944, with FFI personnel marching alongside. The American-built M8 consisted of a 75mm howitzer mounted on an M5 light tank chassis, designed to provide a weight of integral support fire to armoured units. Over 1700 examples were built during World War II.

4 The scene in the town square of Collobrieries, to the east of Toulon, just after liberation by the 1st Free French Division, August 1944.

5 Men of the US 1st Airborne Task Force – a provisional unit scraped together for the landings in southern France and commanded by Major-General Robert T Frederick – jump from C-47 transports over Le Muy to the north of the main assault beaches, 0700 hours, 15 August 1944. Despite the extemporised nature of the Task Force – it had only been put together in July and had never jumped as a complete formation before – the landings were the most accurate and casualty-free of the European campaign.

The Liberation of Paris

1 An American M8 armoured car passes through the Arc de Triomphe, August 1944. The M8 was known in British service as the 'Greyhound' or 'US Greyhound'.

2 French civilians, having come out into the streets to welcome the liberation forces, suddenly find themselves under sniper fire, 25 August 1944.

3 American troops take part in an impromptu victory parade down the Champs Elysées, August 1944.

4 German officers of the Paris garrison are marched into captivity, having suffered the anger of a civilian population which had endured four years of oppression and occupation.

5 As a Sherman of the French 2nd Armoured Division advances warily past the Foreign Ministry (Quai d'Orsay) in Paris, its main turret armament swinging to cover side roads, a civilian Red Cross team rushes to aid the injured.

6 The dramatic scene in the Place de la Concorde, 25 August 1944. Three Shermans of the French 2nd Armoured Division have arrived and the local population has rushed out to greet them, only to come under sniper fire from surrounding buildings.

5

6

Arnhem
War from the sky

1 Parachutes litter the ground as elements of the British 1st Airborne Division land on the outskirts of Arnhem, 17 September 1944. The fact that the LZs (landing zones) were up to 13km (8 miles) outside the town, to the west and northwest, was a crucial factor in the failure to secure the Neder Rijn crossings.

2 British paratroops guard four German prisoners, probably members of the 9th SS Panzer Division *Hohenstaufen*, Arnhem, 17 September 1944. Despite an Allied belief that Arnhem was virtually undefended at the time of Operation Market Garden, two SS Panzer Divisions – the 9th and 10th *Frundsberg* – were in fact in the area, refitting after their defeat in Normandy. The 10th was sent to defend Nijmegen, where it slowed the Allied ground advance, while the 9th, in conjunction with local army units, concentrated on defeating the attack on Arnhem itself.

3 A StuG III Ausf G, with 7·5cm gun, advances along the road to Oosterbeek on 19 September 1944. The photograph was taken in the vicinity of the St Elizabeth Hospital, where men of 2nd Battalion, South Staffordshire Regiment were deployed.

4 British para-gunners fire an American-designed 75mm Pack Howitzer Mark I in the battle for Arnhem, September 1944. This very compact weapon, dismantled into a number of parachute loads or carried complete in a glider, was the main artillery piece available to the British airborne forces in 1944.

5 Arnhem road bridge, photographed after the epic stand by Colonel Frost's men was over, 21 September 1944. German counterattacks had been ferocious since early on 18 September, when a convoy of 16 armoured cars and half-tracks (the remains of which may be seen on the left) tried to clear the bridge from the south, but it was not until late on the 20th, as Tiger tanks of 9th SS Panzer appeared, that the defenders could be dislodged from their positions.

4

5

Chapter 11
The bomber offensive on Germany

1 Marshal of the Royal Air Force Sir Charles Portal (centre, with arm outstretched) visits a barrage-balloon site in southern England, late 1944. As Chief of the Air Staff from 1940 to the end of the war, Portal was a firm advocate of strategic bombing, helping to formulate the British policy of area attacks in 1942 and providing support to Air Chief Marshal Harris as C-in-C Bomber Command.

2 Wing Commander Guy Gibson VC, the dashing young commander of No. 617 Squadron, Bomber Command at the time of the Dams Raid, May 1943. Awarded the Victoria Cross for his work in raising and leading 617 Squadron on this operation, Gibson refused to curtail his operational career. He was killed over Holland in September 1944.

3 Air Chief Marshal Sir Arthur Harris, C-in-C Bomber Command, February 1942 to the end of the war. Appointed at a time when the bombing offensive was at a low ebb, with steady casualties and few results, Harris went on to create a formidable fighting force.

Between 1939 and 1945 over 1,500,000 tons of bombs were dropped onto Germany by Anglo-American air forces in a strategic bombing campaign of mounting ferocity and devastation. It had two basic aims – the precise destruction of German war industries and the undermining of civilian morale – but the achievement of these was fraught with unforeseen problems which made the contribution of the bombers difficult to assess.

The campaign, conducted by Britain alone before August 1942, began badly. The RAF, although firm believers in the theory of victory through air power, lacked aircraft with the range to attack targets deep inside the enemy state. Twin-engined Blenheims, Hampdens, Whitleys and Wellingtons were therefore restricted initially to ineffective night leaflet raids over Germany and daylight attacks on enemy shipping in the North Sea. The latter were disastrous – it was not unknown for 50 per cent of a committed force to be lost to German defences – and from autumn 1940 the offensive was confined largely to night operations.

This produced further problems, for few bomber crews were able to find their targets in the dark. The Butt Report of August 1941 used air photographs, taken as the bombers dropped their loads, to prove that, of the crews who reported hitting a particular location, only about a third had got to within 8 km (5 miles) of it. Precision bombing was clearly impossible and this was tacitly acknowledged on 14 February 1942 when the Area Bombing Directive shifted the bombers away from

surgical strikes, which they could not carry out, to more general attacks upon entire urban areas. If individual factories could not be destroyed, it was now decided to concentrate instead upon the civilian work-force by flattening houses, disrupting normal life and undermining morale.

But cities are enormous targets and it was obvious that a weapon far more powerful than the RAF's existing force was needed. It was the task of Air Marshal Sir Arthur Harris, appointed Commander-in-Chief of Bomber Command on 22 February 1942, to produce such a weapon. He began by restoring confidence in the bombing offensive by means of 'Thousand Bomber' raids, starting with one against Cologne on 30/31 May 1942, and although these had little appreciable effect upon German industry, they boosted British morale and gave Harris political backing for the expansion of his force. He absorbed new equipment – four-engined bombers such as the Stirling, Halifax and Lancaster as well as the versatile twin-engined Mosquito – and supported the use of special radar inventions (Gee, H2S and Oboe) which helped the bombers to find their targets and hit them more accurately.

Once such equipment was available, Harris used it to improve bombing techniques. Through a series of 'battles' – of the Ruhr (March–July 1943), Hamburg (July–November 1943) and Berlin (November 1943–March 1944) – it became normal for more expert crews, known as Pathfinders, to lead the attacks, marking the route and target area

1

for succeeding Main Force waves. Some success was achieved – in late July 1943, for example, Hamburg was devastated by a fire-storm – and precision bombing experiments were resumed, the most notable being the raid on the Ruhr Dams, carried out by 617 Squadron on the night of 16/17 May 1943. But problems remained. Mounting losses, culminating in the Nuremberg raid of 30/31 March 1944 when 97 bombers failed to return, implied that air defence, based upon radar-assisted night-fighters and anti-aircraft guns, was still capable of defeating strategic attacks.

This lesson was also learnt by the Americans, whose Eighth Army Air Force began operations from British airfields in August 1942. Ignoring RAF experience, they persisted in their advocacy of precision bombing and, apparently secure in the development of 'self-defending' bombers such as the B-17 Flying Fortress and B-24 Liberator, insisted on mounting raids deep into Germany during the hours of daylight. They were in for a shock, duly administered by well-organised German defences during raids on ball-bearing factories at Schweinfurt, Bavaria. On two occasions – 17 August and 14 October 1943 – American bombers battled towards this target in broad daylight, eventually losing 96 aircraft to Luftwaffe and ground defences. It was not until the development of a fighter aircraft capable of escorting bombers anywhere in Europe (the P-51D Mustang with Rolls-Royce engine) that the B-17s and B-24s were able to resume operations, but even then it took time (and further losses) before air supremacy could be achieved. The process was not helped by the transfer of Allied heavy bombers to tactical raids in support of the Normandy landings between April and September 1944.

It was not until five years after the war had begun and nearly three years after the American entry that a combined RAF/USAAF bomber offensive could be mounted. But by autumn 1944 the war was nearly over, and although substantial damage was inflicted upon selected cities – notably Dresden in February 1945 – many people were beginning to doubt the efficacy of the campaign. It had taken until late 1944 to produce a viable weapon and the costs – in money, scientific expertise and manpower, all of which might have been better devoted to other aspects of the conflict – were high. The war had clearly not been won by bombing alone and the host of practical problems had blunted its impact. The bomber's survival could not be guaranteed against organised air defences; precision attacks were costly; area bombing was wasteful; and enemy industry and morale had not collapsed.

Such a negative view can be countered, however. The original theory may not have worked in practice, but the destruction imposed undoubtedly prevented a full development of German war industry and, by forcing the enemy to divert resources and manpower to air defence, weakened his front-line strength. The bombers did not win the war, but their contribution to victory was undeniable.

Striking back
The bomber offensive begins

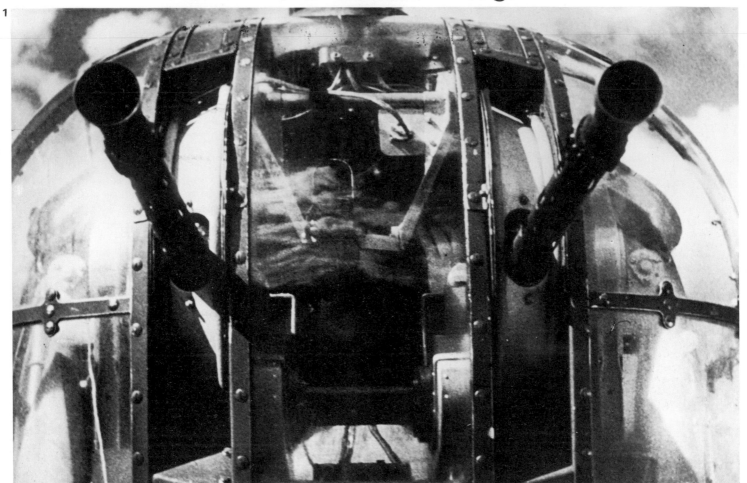

1 Typical bomber armament in the early war years: two .303-inch machine guns in the front turret of a Vickers Wellington III. Designed at a time when fighter aircraft were slow and their threat to the bombers underestimated, such armament proved woefully inadequate during World War II, yet British bombers received few improvements. Even the formidable Stirlings, Halifaxes and Lancasters of the later war years were expected to make do with machine guns which were little more than 'pea-shooters' compared to the cannon of German interceptors.

2 Luftwaffe officers pose alongside the wreckage of a British bomber shot down on the morning of 4 July 1941 at Bremerhaven.

3 A flight of Armstrong-Whitworth Whitley bombers returns from a long-distance reconnaissance patrol over the Frisian Islands.

4 Typical of the bombers in front line squadron service in 1939, the Handley Page Hampden was an unsuitable day-bomber. This photograph shows Hampdens of No. 195 Squadron over the flat land of their home base in Lincolnshire in 1939.

5 Vickers Wellington Is of No. 9 Squadron RAF; a photograph taken in 1939, just prior to the outbreak of war. The Wellington's geodetic construction and sleek lines attracted a great deal of attention but it did not do well in the early months of the war – on 18 December 1939, for example, 24 Wellingtons (including some from No. 9 Squadron) were caught over the North Sea by Bf 109 and Bf-110 fighters and 10 were shot down. The basic Wellington design was sound, however, and subsequent modifications ensured it a place in the night offensive.

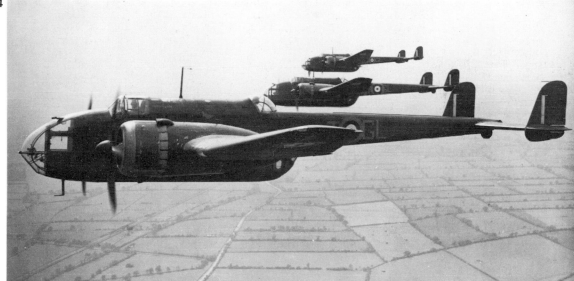

Raiding by night
The RAF over Germany

1 Caught in the camera-flash of an accompanying aircraft, a Handley Page Halifax flies over its target – flying-bomb sites in northern France – 5/6 July 1944. The Halifax, designed initially as a twin-engined aircraft, first flew in its four-engined form in October 1939, entering squadron service in early 1941.

2 Avro Lancaster I, R5868 'S-Sugar', in the colours of No 467 Squadron, Bomber Command, and showing a tally of over 90 operations. This aircraft went on to complete over 140 bombing raids.

3 With its engines at full power, a Lancaster prepares for a night take-off, 1943. Developed initially as the unsuccessful twin-engined Manchester in 1939, the Lancaster, equipped with its four Rolls-Royce Merlin engines, was a superb aircraft.

4 The results of a bombing raid, as interpreted from post-operational air photographs. The target is the oil plant at Wesseling in Gemany, hit in a series of raids between 25 May and 21 July 1944. Damage is shown to (A) a water gas plant, (B) gas holders, (C) a power station, (D) a compressor house and (E) an injector/circulator house.

5 An air-to-air photograph of a Lancaster dropping its bomb load, June 1944.

6 A Short Stirling III of No. 218 Squadron, Bomber Command, stands ready to receive its load of incendiaries, 1942. The Stirling entered front-line service in August 1940.

7 A De Havilland Mosquito bomber, photographed in late 1944. The Mosquito was a remarkable aircraft, developed as a private venture in 1938.

8 A Halifax BIII on a daylight operation over oil installations at Eikel in the Rhur, early 1945.

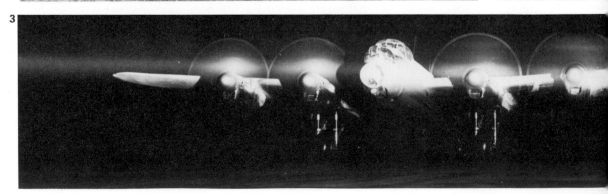

Bombing by day
The American daylight raids

1 North American P-51D Mustang, 'The Millie G', of 343rd Fighter Squadron, 55th Fighter Group, flying out of Little Walden in Hertfordshire as part of the US Eighth Army Air Force (AAF), 1944.

2 Boeing B-17G Flying Fortresses of 303rd Bombardment Group ('Hell's Angels'), 1st Bomb Wing, Eighth AAF, drop bombs onto their target, early 1944. The B-17 first flew (as the Boeing 299) in July 1935 and was designed from the start as a day bomber, able to defend itself against enemy fighters by virtue of its hefty machine-gun fit. Early production models were disappointing but the G model, with its forward-firing chin turret and four 1200hp Wright Cyclone engines, was an effective machine.

3 Caught in the gun-camera of an attacking P-51, a Focke Wulf Fw190 fighter is destroyed over Germany, early 1945.

4 Consolidated B-24J Liberator 'Little Warrior' of 493rd Bombardment Group ('Helton's Hellcats'), 3rd Bomb Wing, Eighth AAF, over Quakenbrück, 29 June 1944. Anti-aircraft fire has ignited the fuel tanks and the aircraft is about to be destroyed.

5 A B-17F, starboard wing destroyed, turns onto its back and spins towards its death, August 1943. Such horrific incidents occurred in the full view of accompanying aircraft, the crews of which must have been deeply affected.

6 B-24s of Eighth AAF fly in mutually-defending 'Box' formation over the Xexia oil refinery at Ploesti, Romania, 1 August 1943. The 179 aircraft involved in this operation flew from bases in North Africa, inflicting considerable damage on the target but losing 52 of their number.

Defence of the Reich
Germany's air defences

1

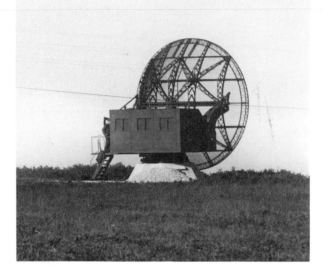

2

1 A 'Giant Würzburg' radar dish, set onto a revolving base, early 1942. The basic Würzburg, produced by Telefunken, was designed in the late 1930s and could secure an accurate fix on aircraft at ranges of up to 40km (25 miles), working on the (then) very high frequency of 560 megacycles. The Giant Würzburg had an extended range of 64km (40 miles)

2 Messerschmitt Bf 110 twin-engined fighters, equipped with FuG 202 Lichtenstein BC air-interception radar for night fighting, photographed on a daylight training mission, 1943. The Lichtenstein had a range of approximately 4km (2·5 miles), the carrying aircraft having to be guided to the general vicinity of the target by ground radar such as the Würzburg.

3 A battery of anti-aircraft guns deployed as part of the defensive ring around a German city, 1942.

4 A Focke Wulf Fw190A day-fighter, photographed in 1942 over Germany. The Fw 190 entered squadron service in 1941 and proved to be a formidable fighting machine in the defence of Germany.

3

4

5

5 8·8cm anti-aircraft fire lights up the night sky over Germany as an RAF raid materialises.

6 A tally of Allied bombers, claimed by the crew of a Würzburg radar set and painted around the central core of the reflector dish. Eleven bombers are claimed, all shot down between July and October 1943.

7 A Junkers Ju 88C-6b, fitted with FuG 202 Lichtenstein BC intercept radar, stands ready on a German airfield, 1943.

8 A Geman night-fighter crew relax over a game of chess while awaiting the order to intercept enemy bombers. The pilot (on the right) is wearing the Knight's Cross of the Iron Cross.

6

7

8

Hamburg
Destruction of a city

1 American bombs fall towards the dockyard areas of Hamburg, 25 July 1943. Although the 'Battle of Hamburg' (24 July–2 August 1943) is usually associated with RAF Bomber Command and the night raids, the US Eighth AAF made a significant contribution on 25 and 26 July, hitting precise targets in daylight and adding to the chaos on the ground. In all, over 50,000 people were killed in the assault on Hamburg.

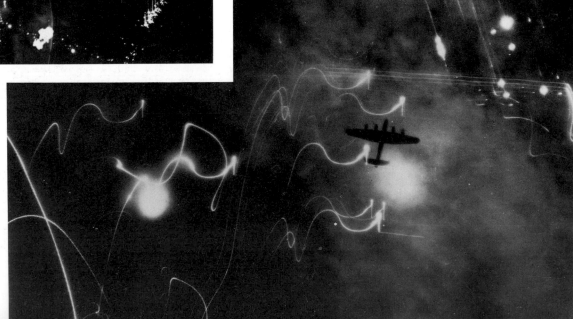

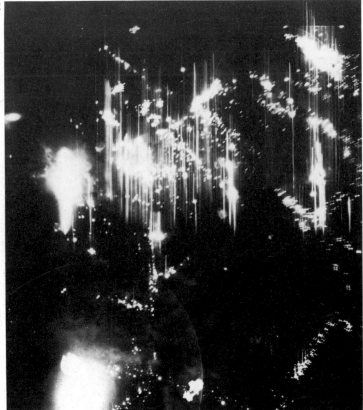

2 A typical scene from the bomb-aimer's position in a night-flying RAF bomber over Hamburg, July–August 1943. The plethora of lights – blurred by the exposure time of the photo-flash – is made up of a combination of incendiary bombs, ground fires and anti-aircraft shells. The bombing is fairly well concentrated – an essential requirement for successful urban destruction.

3 An Avro Lancaster III of Bomber Command in flight, 1943 – a photograph taken during the daily air-test which preceded each raid. Lancasters joined Halifaxes, Stirlings and Wellingtons in hitting Hamburg in late-July/early-August 1943. Only 86 aircraft were lost in 3095 sorties, surprise being achieved through the first use of 'Window' – thin metal strips which swamped enemy radar and made fighter interception impossible.

4 Silhouetted against a background of conflagration and anti-aircraft fire, a Lancaster flies over Hamburg during the night raid of 24/25 July 1943.

5/6 Damage to Hamburg as a result of the raids of late-July/early-August 1943: fire-blackened and gutted buildings stand as mute testimony to the destructive capabilities of Allied bombers.

7 The effects of a fire-storm: civilian bodies litter the streets of Hamburg, August 1943.

Tactical bombing

1 B-24 Liberators of the US Eighth AAF drop their bombs over German positions in the Cotentin Peninsula, preparatory to the American breakout around St Lô, July 1944.

2 The ultimate in Allied ground-attack weapons platforms – a North American B-24H Mitchell, fitted with cannon in the solid nose fairing and fourteen ·50-inch machine guns in nose, side-pack and top turret positions.

3 A Martin B-26 Marauder medium bomber flies over one of the landing beaches in Normandy, June 1944. With a range of 1850km (1150 miles), bomb-load of 1814kg (4000lb), the Marauder was a useful and widely deployed aircraft.

4 B-25C Mitchell medium bombers over the Anzio beach-head, January 1944. The B-25 was one of the most effective interdiction bombers of World War II, enjoying a range of 2052km (1275 miles) and a bomb-carrying capacity of 1814kg (4000lb).

5 A Hawker Typhoon IB of No 486 Squadron, Royal New Zealand Air Force, photographed in 1943, before the introduction of the clear-view 'bubble' canopy. The Typhoon was armed with four 20mm Hispano wing-guns in the B version. Later variants were equipped with eight underwing rockets to give an extremely effective anti-tank punch.

6 A Douglas A-20 Havoc (known in British service as the Boston) flies over a rail junction at Basigny in northern France, 30 April 1944, as part of the highly-successful interdiction campaign, pre D-Day.

7 Bristol Beaufighter Mark IV fighter-bombers attack a German 'flak' (anti-aircraft) ship in the Channel, August 1944, raking it with cannon and rocket fire.

Chapter 12
The end in Europe

1 Marshal Georgi Zhukov, Deputy Supreme Commander in Chief of the Red Army, August 1942 to the end of the war. Famous as the defender of Moscow in late 1941. Zhukov conducted the defence of Stalingrad (1942–43), directed the sweep through Poland (1944) and captured Berlin (1945), although his main role was in helping Stalin to develop strategic plans. He is widely regarded to have been the finest of the wartime Soviet generals.

1

2

Faced with the problems of over-extended supply lines, worsening weather and stiffening resistance from an enemy now fighting on the borders of his homeland, Anglo-American forces in northwest Europe lost momentum late in 1944. By December, despite advances in the south by Patton's US Third Army and Devers' 6th Army Group towards the Saar and into the Vosges Mountains, Montgomery in the north had managed only limited operations to clear the Scheldt estuary and to 'straighten the line' around Venlo, while Bradley in the centre had become bogged down in the Hurtgen Forest and flooded Roer Valley to the east of Aachen. A stalemate had developed and seemed likely to persist until the spring.

Hitler was determined to regain the initiative, using the lull to regroup his forces in the west and to prepare a surprise attack through the weakly defended Ardennes. He scraped together 24 divisions (10 of them armoured) and, in an operation code-named *Wacht am Rhein*, launched them against elements of Hodges' US First Army on 16 December along a 97 km (60 mile) front between Monschau and Echternach. The plan was for the tanks of Sixth SS Panzer and Fifth Panzer Armies, supported on their left by the infantry of Seventh Army, to cross the Meuse River and capture Antwerp in a Blitzkrieg advance which would split the Allied forces in two.

The Americans were caught by surprise and, denied air cover because of low cloud, could do little to prevent an initial breakthrough. But the shoulders of the developing salient or 'bulge' held firm and, as isolated American units defended key locations – notably St Vith (17–22 December) and Bastogne (encircled and besieged, 20–26 December) – the Panzers could not build up the momentum they needed. As Eisenhower reacted by rushing reserves to contain the 'bulge', some German tanks did manage to approach the Meuse

at Dinant (22 December), but as their fuel supplies dwindled and clearing skies allowed Allied fighter-bombers to be deployed, the offensive petered out. By Christmas, with Montgomery preparing counter-attacks from the north and Patton advancing to relieve Bastogne from the south, the tide had begun to turn. A month later, after heavy fighting in winter conditions, the 'bulge' was pinched out and the bulk of the German forces destroyed. At the same time a similar German offensive in northern Alsace (Operation *Nordwind*), launched on 1 January 1945 to relieve Allied pressure in the Ardennes, was also defeated.

Eisenhower, aware that the enemy had been decisively weakened, ordered an immediate advance to the Rhine, aiming to clear the area to the west of the river before authorising assault crossings by Montgomery in the north and Patton in the south. It was a successful move against disorganised German defences. By early March Montgomery's Anglo-Canadians had fought through the Reichwald to close to the Rhine opposite Wesel in Operation 'Veritable', linking up with General Simpson's US Ninth Army which, despite problems crossing the Roer, secured the area from Wesel to Dusseldorf in Operation 'Grenade'. To the south 12th Army Group conducted a broad advance, code-named 'Lumberjack', to clear the Rhine from Cologne down to Mannheim, while 6th Army Group pushed north from Strasbourg to link up with the 12th Army Group. Nor was this all, for on 7 March forward elements of Hodges' First Army, in a remarkable *coup de main*, seized an intact railway bridge across the river at Remagen.

The Americans were quick to exploit the Remagen breakthrough, pouring all available units across the river to consolidate the bridgehead, but this did not preclude the planned assault crossings elsewhere. On 22 March Patton made his move at Nierstein and 24 hours later Montgomery's carefully prepared attack went in around Rees. Both were successful, enabling other crossings to be made all along the Rhine as German defences crumbled. Eisenhower ordered the offensive to continue deep into Germany, with the aim of linking up with Soviet forces from the east on the Elbe River. By early May Montgomery had encircled and cleared the Ruhr industrial area, advanced into northern Holland and taken positions as far to the east as Hamburg and Lübeck; in the centre Bradley had pushed to the Elbe, making contact with the Russians at Torgau on 25 April; in the south Patton and Devers had advanced into Bavaria, western Czechoslovakia and Austria, linking up with forces from Italy on 4 May. On the same

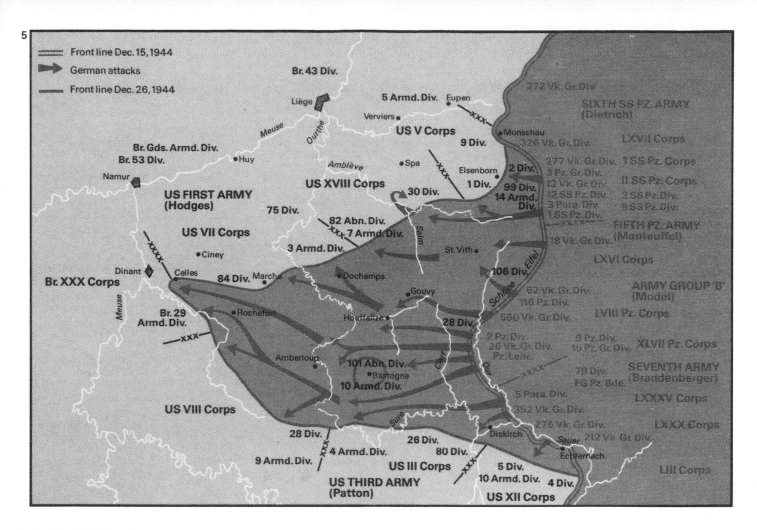

Front line Dec. 15, 1944
German attacks
Front line Dec. 26, 1944

Br. 43 Div.

272 Vk. Gr. Div.

SIXTH SS PZ. ARMY
(Dietrich)

Liège

5 Armd. Div. Eupen

Verviers

US V Corps

Monschau

LXVII Corps

9 Div.

326 Vk. Gr. Div.

Meuse
Ourthe

Br. Gds. Armd. Div.
Br. 53 Div.

Huy

 Amblève

Spa

Elsenborn

2 Div.

277 Vk. Gr. Div.
3 Pz. Gr. Div.
12 Vk. Gr. Div.

1 SS Pz. Corps

Namur

US XVIII Corps

30 Div.

1 Div.

99 Div.
14 Armd.
Div.

12 SS Pz. Div.
3 Para. Div.
1 SS Pz. Div.

II SS Pz. Corps
2 SS Pz. Div.
9 SS Pz. Div.

US FIRST ARMY
(Hodges)

75 Div.

82 Abn. Div.
7 Armd. Div.

Salm

St. Vith

18 Vk. Gr. Div.

FIFTH PZ. ARMY
(Manteuffel)

US VII Corps

Ciney

3 Armd. Div.

Eifel

LXVI Corps

Dinant

Celles

84 Div. Marche

Dochamps

106 Div.

Schnee

ARMY GROUP 'B'
(Model)

Br. XXX Corps

Gouvy

62 Vk. Gr. Div.
116 Pz. Div.

LVIII Pz. Corps

Meuse

Br. 29
Armd. Div.

Rochefort

Houffalize

560 Vk. Gr. Div.

28 Div.

Amberloup

Clerf

2 Pz. Div.
26 Vk. Gr. Div.
Pz. Lehr.

9 Pz. Div.
15 Pz. Gr. Div.

XLVII Pz. Corps

Our

101 Abn. Div.

79 Div.
FG Pz. Bde.

SEVENTH ARMY
(Brandenberger)

Bastogne

10 Armd. Div.

5 Para. Div.

LXXXV Corps

US VIII Corps

352 Vk. Gr. Div.

Sure

276 Vk. Gr. Div.

LXXX Corps

28 Div.

26 Div.

Diekirch

Sauer 212 Vk. Gr. Div.

9 Armd. Div.

4 Armd. Div.

80 Div.

Echternach

LIII Corps

US III CORPS

5 Div.

US THIRD ARMY
(Patton)

10 Armd. Div. 4 Div.

US XII Corps

---

2 The Allied 'Big Three' at Tehran, November 1943. From left to right (seated): Josef Stalin of the Soviet Union, Franklin D. Roosevelt of the USA and Winston Churchill of Britain. These were the men who formulated the grand strategy of the Allied war; their co-operation was not to survive into the peacetime period.

3 One of the last known photographs of Adolf Hitler, taken in the grounds of the Chancellery building in Berlin, March 1945, as he awards boys of the Hitler Youth with the Iron Cross.

4 General Jacob Devers (right), commander of the Sixth Army Group in Europe, attends a conference with General Brehon Somervell, commanding general US Army Service Forces, January 1945. The importance of supply was paramount and Somervell's job – assessing the priority of supply in all theatres of war – was not an enviable one.

5 The Battle of the Bulge.

day, German plenipotentiaries approached the Allies about surrender.

Given the situation on the Eastern Front, this was hardly surprising. Budapest had fallen on 13 February, and despite a desperate counter-attack around Lake Balaton in early March, nothing could stop the Russian steamroller from advancing as far as Vienna by 14 April. The emphasis then shifted to the centre, where Marshals Zhukov and Konev had been building up supplies for a final push from the Oder River to Berlin. The offensive began on 16 April, using overwhelming force, and although German defenders managed to contain the initial bridgeheads across the Oder, by the 20th the breakthrough had occurred. As Marshal Rokossovsky thrust towards the Baltic coast in the north, Zhukov and Konev encircled Berlin, linking up to the west on 25 April before turning inwards to clear the city. It was a bitter house-to-house battle, increasing in intensity as the Russians approached the last bastions of Nazi power around the Reichstag. Hitler, trapped in his bunker beneath the Chancellery, committed suicide on 30 April and two days later Berlin fell. It was a signal for the acceptance of unconditional surrender. The documents were signed on 7 May, and although fighting was to continue until the 11th in Czechoslovakia, where a popular uprising helped the Allies to destroy the remains of the German forces, the war in Europe was over.

Battle of the Bulge
Hitler's final gamble

1 A PzKpfw VI Tiger II (Ausf B) 'Koenigstiger' of an SS Panzer Division carries paratroopers of a Luftwaffe field unit through the forests of the Ardennes, northern sector, 16 December 1944. The Tiger II was a huge and formidable machine, weighing 68 tonnes and armed with an 8·8cm Kwk 43 L/71 main gun.

2 American gunners await the arrival of German armour in a village in the Ardennes, December 1944. Their 57mm M1 anti-tank gun is rather exposed but commands a good field of fire, covering a narrow road along which the enemy would be likely to advance.

3 Supplies are dropped to American troops around Bastogne, late-December 1944. By now the weather had changed from the mud of the early part of the battle to snow and clear skies, enabling Allied air power to be fully deployed.

4 American armour prepares to counterattack in the snow around Houffalize during the actions to squeeze out the 'bulge' in early-January 1945. The two tanks nearest the camera are M4 Shermans with 75mm main armament; the one in the background is an M4A3 variant with redesigned turret and 76mm gun.

5 Panzergrenadiers of 1st SS Panzer Division *Leibstandarte Adolf Hitler* advance through the remains of an American column, 18 December 1944. The photograph – one of a series showing the same men – was probably taken near Poteau, where elements of the US 7th Armored Division were fighting to keep open an escape route from St Vith. It is interesting to note that the grenadier on the right is carrying a captured US M1 carbine.

6 The remains of a PzKpfw IV on the approaches to Bastogne, late-December 1944. The degree of damage implies an air rather than ground attack, emphasising the importance of Allied air power.

Crossing the Rhine
The Allies move into Germany

1 The scene during the night of 23/24 March 1945, as Montgomery's carefully prepared assault crossing of the Rhine at Rees gets under way. Tracer rounds criss-cross the sky as searchlights create 'artificial moonlight' by reflecting their beams off the low cloud base.

2 A glider LZ (landing zone) near Wesel, 24 March 1945. The airborne landings for Montgomery's assault were the responsibility of General Ridgway's XVIII Airborne Corps, comprising the British 6th and US 17th Airborne Divisions. This photograph shows the types of glider used: at the bottom left is a British-built Airspeed Horsa, distinguished by its slightly swept wings and starboard-swinging nose door; eleswhere are the straight-winged American Waco CG-4A Hadrian models.

3 American soldiers of the 89th Division, part of Patton's Third Army, crouch low in their amphibious assault craft as they come under enemy fire while crossing the Rhine. at Oberwesel.

4 With a broken bridge in the background, American infantrymen step onto the east bank of the Rhine, late-March 1945.

5 The Ludendorff railway bridge at Remagen, captured by men of Task Force Engeman, Combat Command B, US 9th Armored Division on 7 March 1945. This photograph, taken from the east bank, shows American armour and infantry.

6 American paras, members of the US 17th Airborne Division, board a C-46 Commando transport aircraft, March 1945.

7 Allied trucks cross a pontoon bridge over the Rhine, early-April 1945. The ability to build pontoons quickly was a major Allied advantage.

Germany's new technology
Jet aircraft and the V weapons

1 A V1 flying bomb, its fuel exhausted, drops like a stone onto London, July 1944. First tested in 1942 and first launched against London on 15 June 1944, the *Vergeltungswaffe Eins* (Reprisal Weapon One) was a pilotless bomb with an 850kg (1870lb) warhead powered by a 600lb thrust Argus As 014 ram-jet which had a very distinctive pulsating sound.

2 A Dornier Do 335 *Pfeil* ('Arrow') at Rechlin airfield, May 1944. This was a highly unorthodox aircraft design, with a propeller at either end of the fuselage.

4

3 A V1 flying bomb in flight, 1944. Over 35,000 V1s were built during the war, of which 9251 were launched against southern England in the second half of 1944.

4 Arado Ar 234B-1/b, Work Number 140312, captured in 1945 and flown to the United States for evaluation. The Ar 234, known as the *Blitz* ('Lightning'), was a twin-engined jet bomber – the first of its kind in the world – which first flew in June 1943.

5 A dramatic photograph of a Spitfire alongside a V1 in flight over the Channel, summer 1944.

6 A captured Messerschmitt Me 262 *Schwalbe* ('Swallow'). The twin-engined Me 262 was the world's first operational jet aircraft, and with a top speed of 868km/h (540mph), it represented an enormous jump in aerial technology.

7 A V2 liquid-fuelled surface-to-surface missile is prepared for launching. The V2 was capable of carrying a one-ton warhead a distance of about 190km (120 miles).

Battle for Berlin

1 'Josef Stalin' (JS) heavy tanks advance into Berlin, May 1945. The JS design, first developed in 1942 in answer to improving German tanks and anti-tank weapons entered service with the Soviet Army in 1943, initial JS-1 models mounting an 85mm or 100mm main gun. The JS-2, with 122mm gun, followed in October 1943 and the final wartime version was the JS-3 with formidable 152mm armament.

2 A Soviet 122mm Model 1931/37 howitzer lays down high-angle fire amid the ruins of Berlin, early-May 1945. The Model 1931/37 – a 122mm Model 1931 field gun barrel mounted on a 152mm Gun-Howitzer Model 1937 carriage – was a sound and reliable gun which saw wide service in Soviet artillery units. It could send its 25kg (55lb) shell to 20,400m (22,320 yds) and was capable (as shown) of elevation to 65 degrees.

3 Ilyushin Il-2m3 Shturmovik ground-attack aircraft fly over the ruins of Berlin, May 1945.

4 A Soviet soldier, steadied by a colleague, attaches the Red Flag to a rather exposed position on top of the *Reichstag* building, Berlin, 2 May 1945.

5 Even the Soviets were surprised at the youth of some of the defenders of Berlin. Here a group of Hitler Youth, probably not yet in their teens, has been extracted from a line of prisoners.

6 The end of the Hitler dream: a local *Gauleiter* (party leader) in Berlin, complete with *Volkssturm* ('home guard') armband, has committed suicide, having first defaced his portrait of the Führer.

7 Soviet soldiers from Asia perform their ablutions in the ruins of a Berlin street, surrounded by the weapons of victory, May 1945. On the left is a line of T-34/85 battle tanks, while the soldiers stand alongside a self-propelled gun.

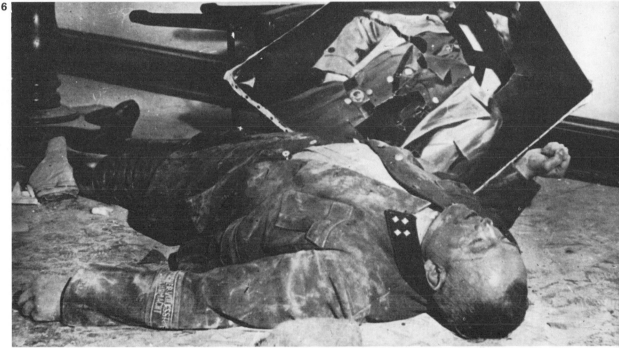

6

7

Victory in the West
The German surrender

1 The Allies link up: American soldiers of General Hodges' First Army shake hands across the remains of a bridge with representatives of the Soviet Fifth Guards Army, Torgau on the Elbe River, 25 April 1945.

2 An indication of Germany's desperation: young boys, no more than 14 or 15 years old, are captured by advancing Allied troops, April 1945. The mixture of dress implies they were in the Hitler Youth.

3 Watched by Admirals Wagner (left) and von Friedeburg (centre), Field Marshal Montgomery reads the surrender terms, Luneburg Heath, 4 May 1945. Montgomery insisted that all enemy units on his northern and western flanks (in northern Holland and Denmark) should be included in the surrender.

4 Two rather aged (and clearly relieved) members of the *Volkssturm* in Allied hands, April 1945. The *Volkssturm* was formed by Hitler's decree on 25 September 1944 and included all available males between the ages of 16 and 60. No uniform was worn but, rather like the early Local Defence Volunteers in Britain in 1940, an armband was issued, in this case (as shown) reading *Deutscher Volkssturm Wehrmacht*. Units were organised at local levels and, in East Prussia particularly, they saw hard fighting.

5 The desperation of defeat: as Allied forces advanced deep into Germany from all sides, Hitler authorised special 'drum-head courts-martial' teams to root out all signs of military weakness. Any soldier found away from his unit without good reason or suspected of a defeatist attitude could be tried on the spot and, if found guilty (often a foregone conclusion), executed as a warning to others – like the one here.

Chapter 13
The fall of Japan

1 Admiral Chester Nimitz, C-in-C of the US Pacific Fleet, December 1941 to the end of the war. The victor of Midway (June 1942), Nimitz went on to command and conduct the campaign in the Central Pacific, leapfrogging amphibious and naval forces from island chain to island chain as far as Okinawa and Iwo Jima in early 1945. It was the largest theatre of operations in World War II, demanding organisational skills which Nimitz amply provided.

2 The end in the Far East: British troops in southern Burma watch as Japanese officers – General Takazo Numato (wearing glasses) and Rear-Admiral Kaigye Chudo – arrive at their headquarters to finalise surrender terms.

3 General Douglas MacArthur, Supreme Commander of the Southwest Pacific Area, announces the liberation of the Philippines, 1945. Promoted to command all US Army units in the Pacific in April 1945, MacArthur took the surrender of Japan aboard the battleship *Missouri* in Tokyo Bay on 2 September after a four-year campaign.

4 The US invasion of Okinawa.

The pressure upon Japan, applied with growing intensity during 1943 and 1944, built up to a crescendo in 1945. Allied forces under General MacArthur in the Philippines, Admiral Nimitz in the central Pacific and General Slim in Burma (the latter as part of Lord Louis Mountbatten's Southeast Asia Command) combined with air and naval activity to destroy the last vestiges of the Japanese imperial dream. It was a hard-fought and costly campaign, but one which Japan could never win.

In Burma Slim began the year facing substantial Japanese forces across the Irrawaddy River. Fearing a trap if he attempted a frontal assault in the north against Mandalay, he concentrated his effort further south, aiming to seize Meiktila and sever the enemy's line of communication to Rangoon. The plan worked well: Meiktila fell to the 17th Indian Division on 3 March and although the Japanese responded by laying siege to the town (15 March), they could do so only by denuding defences elsewhere. This enabled the 19th Indian Division to take Mandalay (20 March), relieve Meiktila (29 March) and force the Japanese to withdraw. Slim pursued them down the Irrawaddy and Sittang Rivers towards Rangoon, bringing other units round by sea from Arakan to take the enemy in the rear. Rangoon fell on 3 May, after which Japanese resistance in Burma crumbled. Slim prepared for his next move – the liberation of Malaya – but the war ended before it could be put into effect.

Meanwhile MacArthur had wasted no time in exploiting his victories in and around Leyte. After preliminary air and naval bombardment, two American corps landed in Lingayen Gulf on the main Philippine island of Luzon (9 January 1945), pushing inland against significant Japanese resistance which included yet more *kamikaze* attacks upon the invasion fleet. Further landings took place between 29 January and 4 February to the north and south of Manila Bay, and as the two invasion forces linked up, Manila was encircled (22 February) and the fortress of Corregidor recaptured (27 February). Manila was strongly defended and had to be taken house by house in a destructive operation which lasted until 3 March. But the campaign did not end there – indeed, it was still going on when Japan surrendered in August – and although the smaller Philippine islands were cleared with comparative ease, the battle for Luzon continued to cause enormous casualties. By August 1945 over 190,000 Japanese and nearly 8000 Americans had been killed.

Nimitz resumed his advance on 19 February 1945 when, after a 72-day air and three-day naval bombardment, two Marine divisions stormed ashore on the small island of Iwo Jima. A beach-

head was established, but after only 20 minutes the Japanese garrison, well-protected in prepared positions, opened up with a withering barrage. The Marines pressed forward, suffering heavy casualties, and split the island in two before turning south to clear Mount Suribachi. It took three days of savage fighting (20–23 February) before the Stars and Stripes could be raised on the summit and another month of combat to take the rest of the island. When the operation ended on 26 March almost 22,000 Japanese and 7000 Americans had lost their lives.

By then Nimitz had already turned to his next objective – the island of Okinawa in the Ryukyu group, an integral part of Japan itself. The preliminary bombardment began on 14 March and on 1 April two American corps landed on the west coast of the island, advancing inland against stiffening resistance. Most of the island had been cleared by 13 April, but in the far south the prepared defences of the Shuri Line caused problems which were not overcome until 21 May. Even then the campaign was to take another month to complete, with casualties rising all the time: by 21 June over 100,000 Japanese and 12,000 Americans were dead.

Such sobering losses made it obvious that an invasion of the main Japanese islands was going to be hideously expensive (the Americans estimated up to a million Allied casualties) and although plans were made for landings on Kyushu in November (Operation 'Olympic') and around Tokyo in March 1946 (Operation 'Coronet'), alternative methods of forcing Japan to surrender were clearly needed. Fortunately these already existed, for as the land campaigns crept closer to Japan, naval and air operations began to have an effect. On the naval side a sustained campaign against Japanese trade, using submarines, mines, surface warships and carrier-borne aircraft, gradually destroyed substantial elements of the enemy's mercantile marine, cutting Japan off from her resource areas and shattering her economy. At the same time, a strategic bombing campaign, mounted initially from bases in central China (May–December 1944) and then from the newly-liberated Mariana Islands (November 1944–August 1945), hit Japanese cities and destroyed industrial capacity. Using specially designed B-29 Superfortress long-range bombers,

the campaign enjoyed mounting success, particularly when the emphasis was switched from daylight precision to night-time incendiary attacks. Tokyo was devastated by a fire-storm on 9/10 March 1945 and by July the B-29s had virtually run out of worthwhile targets.

The Japanese still showed no signs of surrender, however, and US President Harry Truman turned to new technology. On 16 July 1945 scientists of the Manhattan Project had exploded an atomic device at Alamagordo, New Mexico, and on 6 August the first atomic bomb was dropped by a B-29 onto the Japanese city of Hiroshima. The results were horrific – over 70,000 people died – but still the Japanese would not give in. It was to take a Soviet declaration of war and invasion of Manchuria (8–18 August), as well as a second atomic strike, this time on Nagasaki (9 August), for the Japanese finally to accept the inevitable. On 15 August Emperor Hirohito broadcast his decision to surrender and on 2 September Japanese representatives signed the surrender on board the American battleship *Missouri* in Tokyo Bay. World War II was over.

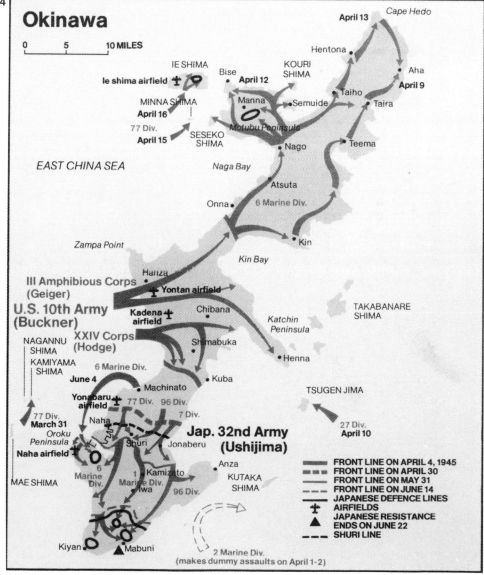

Iwo Jima

1 One of the most famous and evocative photographs of World War II: American Marines raise the 'Stars and Stripes' at the summit of Mount Suribachi, 1020 hours, 23 February 1945. This was in fact the second flag to be raised – the first was too small to be seen from the beaches – and this enabled Associated Press photographer Joe Rosenthal to catch the moment for posterity.

2 With the 167m (546 ft) Mount Suribachi (an extinct volcano) in the background, landing ships make for the beaches, Iwo Jima, 19 February 1945. The assault was carried out by Major-General Harry Schmidt's V Amphibious Corps (4th and 5th Marine Divisions, with 3rd Marine Division in reserve) and was intended to take both Suribachi and one of the two airfields on the island (Motoyama No. 1) by the end of the first day. Despite landing some 30,000 Marines, neither objective was taken against fanatical Japanese resistance.

3 Japanese soldiers lie dead in a shell crater, Iwo Jima, March 1945. Of the garrison of 22,000 men, nearly all were killed in the savage fighting which was needed to secure the island. Even when the battle was lost, many Japanese soldiers – of whom the two in this photograph were probably part – chose to commit suicide rather than endure the humiliation of captivity.

4 A scene on the landing beach, Iwo Jima, 19 February 1945. Despite a massive preliminary air and naval bombardment, the Japanese garrison was still effective when the landings took place.

5 A wounded Marine is helped on board an evacuation vessel, Iwo Jima, February 1945. By the end of the Iwo Jima battle in mid-March, the Americans had lost nearly 7000 dead and over 17,000 wounded – a high cost. However, they had gained an island within fighter-aircraft range of Japan itself, substantially increasing the pressure on the enemy power.

Kamikaze
The divine wind

1

1 A Nakajima B6N2 carrier-borne attack bomber (Allied code-name 'Jill') on a *kamikaze* (suicide) mission veers away from an American warship, its port wing shattered by cannon fire: a photograph taken during the fierce fighting off Okinawa, early-April 1945.

2 In the aftermath of a *kamikaze* strike, the aft section of an American carrier burns fiercely. The first organised *kamikaze* mission (six aircraft) took off from Cebu in the Philippines late on 25 October 1944. Arriving over Leyte Gulf two hours later, the planes deliberately rammed the US carriers *Santee* and *Suwanee*, badly damaging both ships. The next day a second mission sank the carrier *St Lô* in the same area.

3 A Mitsubishi A6M Zero flies through a barrage of anti-aircraft fire as its pilot tries to ram the battleship USS *Missouri*, early-1945.

4 As crew members of an American escort carrier watch, a landing ship explodes under *kamikaze* attack, off the Ryukyu Islands.

2

3

4

5 Japanese naval pilots pose beside a Mitsubishi A6M Zero fighter, Rabaul, 1942. It was men such as these who accepted the daunting task of conducting *kamikaze* missions. Interestingly, the pilot standing, top row, left is Saburo Sakai, Japan's third ranking and most senior surviving fighter pilot of the war, with 64 'kills' to his credit. He began his combat career in China in 1938 and participated in all the early air operations of the Pacific War before being badly wounded over Guadalcanal in August 1942. He even took part in a *kamikaze* mission, only to be intercepted by American fighters and forced to turn back.

6 The best defence against *kamikaze* attack was to put up an enormous barrage of anti-aircraft fire. This photograph, taken aboard a US carrier off Okinawa in April 1945, shows the crew of a 40mm Quad AA gun in the midst of battle.

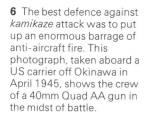

MacArthur returns
American invasion of the Philippines

1 US troops of the American Division wade ashore across heavily-mined beaches, during the invasion of Cebu Island, March 1945.

2 Armed with M1 carbines US soldiers come under fire from Japanese positions along the shore-line. By 1945 the Americans were experts in amphibious warfare: the assault troops were equipped with amphibious vehicles while the attack itself would be preceded by massive aerial and naval bombardments.

3 Preferring death to dishonour, this Japanese soldier on the Philippines has committed ritual suicide with his bayonet. While the bravery of the Japanese armed forces was universally acknowledged by the Americans and British, the archaic Japanese attitude towards honour in battle was often detrimental to basic military efficiency.

4 A converted M4 Sherman tank fires a blast of flame at a Japanese position on the Philippines. Flame-throwers were useful weapons for winkling-out Japanese defenders in bunkers and other fortified strong points.

5 Soldiers of the XI corps fire an M115 8-inch howitzer against remaining pockets of Japanese resistance on Ipo Dam Hill, May 1945. The M115 howitzer was a heavy weapon capable of firing a projectile weighing 92kg (200lb), and had a range of 16,800m (18,370 yds).

6 A scene of devastation in Manila, the capital city of the Philippines. In marked contrast to most of the island campaigns fought by the Americans, the re-taking of the Philippines involved fighting over urban areas with the attendant problems of civilian casualties and material destruction. In order to keep their own casualties to a minimum, the Americans relied on the application of massive firepower to destroy the defending Japanese.

4

5

6

Victory in Burma

1 Japanese troops cross the Chindwin River during the build-up for their attack on Imphal-Kohima, early 1944. The photograph gives some idea of the problems posed by the rivers of Burma, with their strong currents and great width.

2 British commandos, supported by M4 Sherman tanks, advance across Akyab Island, Arakan, January 1945. Despite the failure of the Arakan operations in 1942 and 1943, a third attack – Operation Talon – was mounted in December 1944. With the main Japanese force in Burma under pressure on the Irrawaddy River, the advance towards Akyab and Ramree was successful, using a series of coast-hopping amphibious landings to secure key locations. Troops from Arakan were used in Operation Dracula (early-May 1945) to attack Rangoon from the sea.

3 Men of the 11th (East African) Division march towards Kalewa on the Chindwin River during the pursuit of Japanese forces defeated at Imphal-Kohima, August 1944. Composed of men of the King's African Rifles and Northern Rhodesia Regiment, the division was only one of a number of formations raised in Britain's African colonies which saw service in Burma.

4 A corporal of the 25th Indian Division fires his Thompson sub-machine gun at Japanese positions during the advance in Arakan, January 1945.

5 A Sherman of B Squadron, King George V's Own 19th Lancers – an Indian Army unit – advances to take up a fire-position in hilly terrain, Kabaw Valley, September 1944. Although Burma was not ideal tank country, the Shermans proved useful in providing fire support, and once the breakthrough at Meiktila had occurred in March 1945, tanks were able to move into more open country on the road to Rangoon.

6 Soldiers of the 19th Indian Division take up defensive positions on the outskirts of Mandalay, March 1945. The man on the right is firing a ·303-inch Bren light machine gun.

Death from the sky
The strategic air offensive on Japan

1 A specially-modified B-25B Mitchell medium bomber struggles into the air from the deck of the carrier USS *Hornet*, 18 April 1942. 16 such aircraft, commanded by Lieutenant Colonel James H Doolittle, were launched to fly 620 nautical miles to Tokyo, which they bombed from 450m (1500 ft) before flying on to bases in China.

2 Bombs rain down on the already-burning coastal city of Takamatsu on the Japanese island of Shikoku, 4 July 1945.

3 An aerial photograph, taken after the war was over, of the centre of Tokyo, showing the extent of the fire damage inflicted in a series of incendiary raids (25 February, 9/10 March and 25 May).

4 Against a backdrop of towering clouds, B-29s fly towards Japan, early 1945. Designed and built specifically for very long range operations against Japan, the first B-29 took to the air on 21 September 1942.

5 Colonel Paul W Tibbetts, commander of the 509th Composite Group, waves from the cockpit of the most famous B-29 of all – 44-86292 'Enola Gay'. It was this aircraft, flown by Tibbetts, which at 0816 hours on 6 August 1945 dropped the first atomic bomb, on the Japanese city of Hiroshima. Producing an explosion equivalent to 20,000 tons of TNT, the bomb – codenamed 'Little Boy' – killed approximately 78,000 people and injured a further 51,000.

6 The results of the second atomic raid, carried out against Nagasaki just before 1100 hours on 9 August 1945.

7 Incendiary bombs fall onto the dockyards of Kobe on the island of Honshu, 5 June 1945. Already devastated by a night incendiary attack on 16/17 March, Kobe was virtually destroyed by the raid of 5 June.

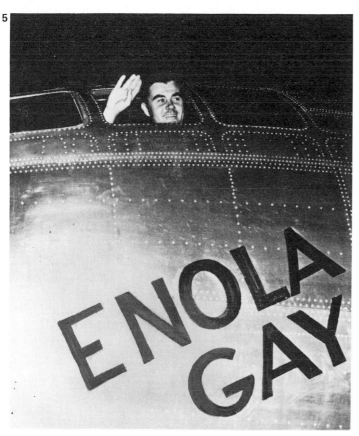

Victory in the East
The Japanese surrender

1 With an American soldier in the background, Japanese prisoners of war smash equipment in a military depot in Japan, September 1945. They appear to be using the remains of a light anti-aircraft gun as an 'anvil' upon which to break off the stocks of their Arisaka rifles.

2 The symbol of Allied victory: Corporal Charles Dunn raises the 'Stars and Stripes' over the Yokosuka naval base in Japan.

3 Lord Louis Mountbatten discusses the surrender arrangements with his commanders in South East Asia Command (SEAC). From left are General Slim, General Wheeler, Mountbatten, Admiral Power, Air Chief Marshal Sir Keith Park and General Browning. SEAC had to organise the disarming and repatriation of enemy soldiers in areas such as Malaya, Singapore, Borneo, the Dutch East Indies and French Indochina. Allied troops were to be involved in all such areas.

4 The moment the war officially ended. General Douglas MacArthur, already named as commander of occupation forces in Japan, signs the document of Japanese surrender aboard the American battleship *Missouri* in Tokyo Bay, 2 September 1945.

5 As crew members of *Missouri* watch from every possible vantage point, Japanese representatives attend the surrender ceremony, 2 September 1945. The man in morning suit and top hat is Mamoru Shigemitsu, newly-appointed Foreign Minister of Japan; on his left stands General Yoshijiro Umezu, Army Chief of Staff. Both were to be tried for war crimes and sentenced to long terms of imprisonment.

6/7 Soviet troops receive an enthusiastic welcome from the citizens of Manchuria, August 1945. The Soviets invaded Manchuria on 9 August, having declared war on Japan the previous night. The campaign lasted only nine days, with armies attacking from north, west and east simultaneously, and although the Japanese had nearly a million men in the country, they were no match for the armour, air power and experience of the Soviet forces, many of whom had fought in the war against Germany. By 18 August the campaign was over.

Index

Numbers in *italics* refer to chapter introductions

Abyssinia *7*, 32–33
Admiral Scheer, battleship 82
Air defence, German 158–59
Alexander, General Sir Harold 71, 120–21
Alps 130–31
Anti-aircraft guns 158
   3·7in 22, 130
   8·8cm 19, 73
   40mm Quad 181
Anti-semitism *7*, 9
Anti-submarine warfare 90–91
Anti-tank guns
   4·7cm Panzerjaeger 52
   5cm Pak 38, 46, 52, 141, 144
   57mm 136, 166
   6-pounder 122
Anzio *120–21*, 121, 128–29, 163
Armoured cars
   M8 142, 146
   SdKfz 222 135
Arnhem *133*, 148–49
Artillery
   5·5in 127, 139
   6in 31
   8in M115 183
   25-pounder 72, 76
   75mm M8 144
   75mm Pack Mark 1 149
   76·2mm Model 1939 99
   105mm M3 113, 115
   10·5cm Leichte Feldhaubitze 18, 38
   203mm Model 1931 99
Artillery tractors 19, 23, 39
HMS *Ashanti*, destroyer 91
SS *Athenia*, passenger liner *82*
Atlantic, Battle of the 82–93
Atomic bomb *6*, *177*
Austria *6–7*, *164*
Azerbaijan, tanker 86

Balkans *28–29*, 34–37, Liberation of *95*, 106–07
Barbarossa *42*, 44–47
Bataan 62
Battle of Britain *11*, 24–25
Battle of the Bulge *165*, 165–67
Belgium *10*, 19
Berlin 9, *164*, 172–73
Bismarck, battleship *83*, 83, 88–89
Blitz, The *11*, 26–27
Bombers
   Aichi D3A 64
   Arado Ar 234B-1/6 171
   Armstrong Whitworth Whitley 153
   Avro Lancaster 154, 160
   B-17 Flying Fortress 59, 151, 156–57
   B-24H Mitchell 162
   B-24J Liberator 157, 162
   B-25 Mitchell *57*, 80, 162, 186
   B-26 Marauder 162
   B-29 Superfortress *177*, 187, 'Enola Gay' 187

De Havilland Mosquito 155
Douglas SBD Dauntless 64–65
Handley Page Halifax 154–55
Handley Page Hampden 153
Heinkel He-111 12, 25–26
Junkers Ju-87 Stuka 18, 45
Nakajima B6N2 162
P-51D Mustang 156
Savoia Marchetti SM-79 40
Savoia Marchetti SM-81 34
Short Stirling III 155
Vickers Wellington I 153
Vickers Wellington III 152
Bombing offensives 150–63
Bradley, General Omar *132–33*, 132, *164*
Britain *6–7*, *10–11*, 24–27, *82–83*
British forces
   Air Force 11, 24–25, *28*, 40, *150–51*, 152–55, 160–61
   Army 14–15, 22–23, 33, *56*, 60, 72–73, 122–25, 176, Western Desert force *28–29*, 31, First Army 80, Eighth Army *29*, *70–71*, 76–77, 120–21, 1st Airborne Division *133*, 148, 11th Division 185, Chindits *108*, 116–17, Special Air Service Brigade 74, Manchester Regiment 15, Royal Artillery 15, Royal Tank Regiment 31, Scottish Regiment 128, Welsh Guards 15, Marines 135–36, 184
   Navy *10*, *28–29*, 61, *82*, 90–91
Brooke-Popham, Air Marshal Sir Robert 56
Browning, General Frederick 188
Budapest 106–07, 164
Budenny, Marshal Semyon 43
Burma *56*, *108*, 116–17, *176*, 184–85

Caen *133*, 138–41
California, battleship 59
Calvert, Colonel Michael 116
Canadian Army
   Anglo-Canadian Second Army *132–33*, 164, 2nd Canadian Division *132*, 135, 139
Cassino *120–21*, 121, 126–27
Cavallero, Marshall Ugo 39
Chamberlain, Neville 6
Chennault, Major-General Claire L. 108
China *56*, *109*, 114–15, *177*
Chinese Nationalist forces
   Air Force 114
   Army 114–15
Chudo, Rear-Admiral Kaigye 176
Churchill, Sir Winston 10–11, *82*, 164
Ciano, Count Galeazzo 6
Clark, General Mark W. *120*, 120
Convoys *82–83*, 86–87
Coral Sea, Battle of the *57*, 64
SS *Coulmore*, merchantman 86
Coventry 27
Crete *29*, 36–37

Czechoslovakia *6–7*, *164*

D-Day landings *132*, 133, 136–37
Dachau concentration camp 9
Daladier, Edward 6
de Gaulle, General Charles 133
Denmark 10
Deutschland, battleship *82*
Devers, General Jacob *133*, *164*, 165
Dieppe *132*, 134–35
Doenitz, Admiral Karl 83
Doolittle, Colonel James *57*
Dunkirk *10*, 22–23

Eagle, aircraft carrier 41
Eisenhower, General Dwight D. 71, *132–33*, 132, *164–65*
El Alamein *70–71*, 76–77
Ethiopian guerrillas 32–33
Europe, Invasion of 132–49

Fighter-bombers
   Bristol Beaufighter Mark IV 163
   Hawker Typhoon IB 139, 163
Fighters
   Curtiss Hawk 114
   Curtiss P40N (Kittyhawk IV) 76
   Dornier Do335 Pfeil (Arrow) 170
   Douglas A-20 Havoc 163
   Focke Wulf Fw 190 156, 158
   Grumman F6F Hellcat 119
   Hawker Hurricane II 24, 41
   Hawker Sea Hurricane IA 'Hurricat' 91
   Junker Ju 88C-6b 159
   Messerschmitt Bf-109 25, 45
   Messerschmitt Bf-110 158
   Messerschmitt Me-262 171
   Mitsubishi A6M Zero 58, 66–67, 181
   P-38 Lightning 80
   P-51D Mustang *151*
   Supermarine Spitfire 24, 40, 171
Finland 10
Flying boats, Short Sunderland 91
France *6–7*, *10–11*, 14–15, 18–23, 28, *132–33*, 134–47
French Army 14–15, 20–23, 131, *133*, 144–45
Freyberg, Major-General Bernard 36

Gamelin, General Maurice 10
Gazala Line *70*, 72–73
Georges, Alphonses 10
German forces
   Air Force *7*, *11*, 12, 24–25, *28–29*, 152, 159, Paratroopers 18, 35–37
   Army *7*, *10*, 11–13, 19, 21, 23, *42–43*, 44–54, 81, *94–95*, 96–97, 100, 102–04, 106, 122, 124, 126, 129–30, *132–33*, 135–36, 140–41, 146–48, 165, Afrika Corps *29*, 38–39, *70–71*
   Condor Legion 7
Gibson, Guy 150

Gliders
   Airspeed Horsa 168
   Waco CG-4a Hadrian 168
Gneisenau, battleship *82*, 82
Gort, General Viscount John 10
Graf Spee, battleship *82*
Graziani, General Rudolfo 71
Greece *28–29*, 34
Greek Army 35
Guadalcanal *57*, 66–67
Guderian, Colonel General Heinz *42*, 95, 132

Halsey, Admiral William *108*, 108
Hamburg, Bombing of *150–51*, 160–61
Harris, Air Chief Marshal Sir Arthur *150*, 151
Hess, Rudolf 8
Himmler, Heinrich 8–9
Hirohito, Emperor *177*
Hiroshima *177*
Hitler, Adolf 6, *7*, 8, *11*, *42–43*, *94*, *164*, 165
Hitler Youth 165, 174
Hodges, General Courtney 164
Hoepner, General Erich *42*
Holland *10*, 18, *164*
Homma, General Masaharu 56
Hong Kong *56*, 114
HMS *Hood*, battlecruiser *83*, 88
USS *Hornet*, aircraft carrier *57*, 186
Hoth, General Hermann *42*, 42
Hungarian Army 107
Hungary *6–7*

Indian Army 33, 116, 131, *176*, 185
Indomitable, aircraft carrier 41
Ironside, General Sir William 10
Italian Army *28*, 30, 32, 34
Italian Campaign 120–31
Iwo Jima *176*, 178–79

Japan *6–7*, Fall of 176–89
Japanese forces
   Army *56*, 60–61, 63, 114, 117, *176*, 179, 182, 184, 188
   Navy *56*, 58, 64, 67, *108–09*, 118–19, 181

Kamikaze attacks *108*, *176*, 180–81
Kesselring, Field Marshal Albert 71, *120*, 120
Kobe dockyards 187
Konev, Marshal Ivan 94, *95*, *164*
Kurita, Vice-Admiral Takeo 109
Kursk *94*, 96–97

Landing craft, infantry (LCI) 78, 136
Landing craft, tank (LCT) 125, 128, 134, 136, 182
Landing Vehicle Tracked (LVT)
   Amtrac 111
   Water Buffalo 112
Layton, Sir Geoffrey 56

League of Nations 6–7
Leningrad, Siege of 95, 100–01
Leyte Islands 108, 118–19, 176
Libya 28–29, 38
London 11, 26–27, 170
Long Range Desert Group 75
Lucas, Major-General John 120
Luneberg Heath, Surrender at 174

MacArthur, General Douglas 56, 108–09, 176, 177, 188
Machine guns
 ·303in Bren 185
 ·50in Browning 74–75, 112, 128
 DP 1928 54, 106
 6·5mm Fiat-Revelli Model 1914 32
 ·303in Lewis 75
 7·92mm MG34 18
 7·92mm MG42 103, 126
 7·7mm Type 92 67
 ·303in Vickers 15, 31
Maginot Line 10, 14–15
Malaya 56, 60–61, 176
Malta 28–29, 40–41
Manchuria 7, 189
Manila 56, 63, 176, 183
Mariana Islands 108, 112–13, 177
Midway, Battle of 57, 65
Mikuma, cruiser 65
Missouri, battleship 177, 188–89
Mitscher, Vice-Admiral Marc 108
Montgomery, General Sir Bernard Law 70 71, 70, 120, 132–33, 132, 164–65, 174
Morshead, Major-General Leslie 28
Mortars
 8·1cm GrW34 124
 82mm Model 1941 106
Moscow 42, 48–49
Mountbatten, Lord Louis 176, 188
Munich Agreement (1938) 6, 28
Mussolini, Benito 6, 28, 120, 121
Mutaguchi, General Renya 57

Nagasaki 177, 186
Nagumo, Vice-Admiral Chuichi 56
Narvik, Battle of 10, 16–17
National Socialists (Nazis) 7, 8–9, 13
New Guinea 109
New Zealand Air Force 163
Nimitz, Admiral Chester 57, 108–09, 176, 176
Normandy 132, 136–37, 142–43, 151, 162
North Africa 28–39, 70–81
Norway 10, 16–17
Numato, General Takazo 176

O'Connor, Major-General Richard 28
Ohio, tanker 41
Okinawa 176, 180–81
HMS Onslow, destroyer 91
Operations
 Anvil 132, 144–45
 Avalanche 120
 Bagration 95
 Barbarossa 42
 Battleaxe 29
 Baytown 120
 Brevity 29
 Cobra 133, 142

Coronet 177
Crusader 29
Dragoon 133, 144–45
Dynamo 10
Epsom 133, 140
Goodwood 133, 138
Grenade 164
Husky 120
Lightfoot 70
Market Garden 133
Nordwind 165
Olympic 177
Overlord 132, 136–37
Sea lion 11
Shingle 120
Slapstick 120
Supercharge 71
Torch 71, 78–79
Totalize 139
Veritable 164
Wacht am Rhein 164
Ozawa, Vice-Admiral Jisaburo 108, 109

Pacific 56–59, 108–19
Paris 10, 21, Liberation of 133, 146–47
Park, Air Chief Marshal Sir Keith 188
Partisans, Soviet 50–51
Patton Jr., General George S. 71, 120, 132, 133, 164–65
Paulus, General Friedrick 43, 43
Pearl Harbor 56, 58–59
Pétain, Marshal Philippe 10
Philippine Sea, Battle of 108, 109
Philippines 56, 62–63, 109, 176, 182–83
PIAT 81
Poland 6–7, 10, 12–13, 102
Polish forces
 Air Force 10
 Army 12–13
 Home Army 95, 104
Portal, Sir Charles 150
Pound, Admiral Dudley 82
Power, Admiral Arthur 188
Prague 7
Prien, Captain Gunther 83
Prince of Wales, battleship 56, 61

Radar 11, 150, 158–59
Raedar, Admiral Erich 83
Ramsay, Admiral Sir Bertram 132
Red Army see Soviet Army
Remagen 164, 169
Repulse, battleship 56
Rhine, River 164–65, 168–69
Rhineland 6–7
Rifles
 ·303in Lee Enfield 33
 ·303in Lee Enfield No.4 72, 123
 ·30in M1 Carbine 182
 ·30in M1 130
 7·92mm Mauser M98K 54
 7·62mm Mosin Nagant 1891/30 97
 ·30in Springfield Model 1903A4 130
Rocket launchers,
 15cm Nebelwerfer 41 141
Rockets
 4·5in M8 112

38cm Sprenggranate 4581 105
HMS Rodney, battleship 139
Rokossovsky, Marshal Konstantin 94, 95, 164
Rome 121, 121, 128–29
Rommel, General Erwin 28, 29, 39, 70–71, 71, 132

Sakai, Saburo 181
Salerno 120, 124–25
USS Sangamon, escort carrier 119
Scharnhorst, battleship 82–83
Shaw, Major Freddie 116
Sherbrooke, Captain R. St. V 82
Shigemitsu, Mamoru 189
Sicily, Invasion of 120, 122–23
Simpson, General William 164
Singapore 56, 60–61
HMS Skate, escort destroyer 90
Slim, General Sir William 108, 108, 176, 188
Solomons 109
Somervell, General Brehon 165
South African Army 32, 72, 120
Soviet Army 42–43, 46–47, 49, 52–55, 94–95, 96–101, 106–07, 164, 174, 189
Soviet Union 42–55, 94–107
Spanish Civil War 7, 7
Stalin, Josef 164
Stalingrad 43, 54–55
Strasser, Gregor 8
Student, General Kurt 36
Surrender of France 21, of Germany 174–75, of Japan 188–89
Sub-machine guns
 9mm MP34 22
 9mm MP38/40 54
 7·62mm PPSh-41 106, 46, 50–51, 54
 ·45in Thompson 123–24, 130

Tank destroyers, M10 144
Tanks
 Churchill 134, 139
 M3 73
 M4 Sherman 77, 128, 138, 143, 147, 166, 183–85
 M5A1 (Stuart IV) 81
 M13/40 30
 Matilda II 31
 PzKpfw III 19, 35, 38, 77, 81
 PzKpfw IV 44, 46, 96, 103, 106, 129
 PzKpfw V Panther 94, 96, 102, 142–43
 PzKpfw VI Tiger 94, 96–97, 102, 106, 129, 140–41, 166–67
 PzKpfw 35(t) 46
 Renault R-35 20
 StuG III Ausf G 48, 125, 148
 T-26 49
 T-34 49, 53, 98, 107
 T-34/76 96–97
 Type 89 63
 Type 95 60
 Type 97 116
Tarawa 109, 110–11
Tedder, Air Chief Marshal Sir Arthur 132
Thailand 56, 60
Tibbetts, Colonel Paul W. 187
Timoshenko, Marshal Semyon 42

Tirpitz, battleship 83, 92–93
Tobruk 29, 70
Tojo, General Hideki 57
Tokyo 177, 186
Torch Landings 71, 78–79
Torpedo-bombers
 Fairey Albacore 41, 92
 Fairey Swordfish 89
Transport planes
 C-46 Commando 169
 C-47 Dakota 117
 Junkers Ju-52 36, 80
 Junkers Ju-52/3 18, 35
Truman, President Harry 177
Tunisia 71, 80–81

U-boats 82–83, 84–85
Umezu, General Yoshijiro 189
United States forces
 Air Force 64–67, 108, 114, 156–57, Eighth Army Air Force 151, 156–57, 160
 Army 62, 78–79, 81, 122–24, 129–30, 146–47, 166, 169, 182–83, First Army 132–33, 136–37, 164, 174, Third Army 133, 142–43, 164, 168, Fifth Army 120–21, Sixth Army 133, 164, Seventh Army 120, 133, Ninth Army 164, First Airborne Task Force 145
 Navy 108, 119, Pacific Fleet 56–57, 58–59
 Marines 57, 66, 109, 110–13, 176, 178–79

V1 flying bomb 170–71
V2 flying bomb 171
Valetta 41
Vasilevsky, General A. M. 94
Versailles peace treaty 6–7
Vichy Government 11, 28
von Bock, Field Marshal Fedor 10, 11, 42, 42
von dem Bach-Zelewski, Erich 95
von Friedeburg, Admiral Hans 174
von Kluge, Field Marshal Gunther 94
von Leeb, Field Marshal Wilhelm 42
von Manstein, Field Marshal Erich 42–43, 94, 94
von Ribbentrop, Joachim 29
von Runstedt, Field Marshal Gerd 10, 42, 132

Wagner, Admiral 174
Warsaw 10, 13, Uprising 95, 104–05
Wavell, General Sir Archibald 56
Wedemeyer, Major-General Albert 108
West Virginia, battleship 38
Western Desert 30–31
Western Front 10, 14–15
Wheeler, General R. A. 188
Wingate, Brigadier Orde 108

Yamato, battleship 118
Yugoslavia 6, 29, 35
Yugoslavian Army 35

Zhukov, Marshal Georgi 94–95, 164, 164
Zuiho, aircraft carrier 118

Bibliography

C. Barnett, *The Desert Generals* (William Kimber, 1960)

A. Bullock, *Hitler: A Study in Tyranny* (Odhams, 1952)

A. Calder, *The People's War: Britain, 1939–1945* (Jonathan Cape, 1969)

A. Clark, *Barbarossa: The Russian-German Conflict, 1941–45* (Hutchinson, 1965)

J. Costello and T. Hughes, *The Battle of the Atlantic* (William Collins, 1977)

W. Craig, *The Fall of Japan* (Penguin, 1979)

J. Ellis, *The Sharp End of War: The Fighting Man in World War II* (David and Charles, 1980)

T. Harrisson, *Living through the Blitz* (Collins, 1976)

M. Hastings, *Bomber Command* (Michael Joseph, 1979)

W. G. F. Jackson, *The Battle for Italy* (Batsford, 1967)

B. H. Liddell Hart, *The Other Side of the Hill; Germany's Generals, their rise and fall, with their own account of military events, 1939–1945* (Cassell, 1948)

B. H. Liddell Hart, *History of the Second World War* (Cassell, 1970)

F. K. Mason, *Battle over Britain* (McWhirter Twins, 1969)

R. J. Overy, *The Air War, 1939–1945* (Europa, 1980)

T. Parrish (ed), *The Encyclopedia of World War II* (Secker and Warburg, 1978)

A. Preston (ed), *Decisive Battles of the Pacific War* (Hamlyn, 1979)

A. J. P. Taylor, *The Origins of the Second World War* (Hamish Hamilton, 1961)

J. Toland, *But Not in Shame* (Gibbs and Phillips, 1962)

R. F. Weigley, *Eisenhower's Lieutenants: The Campaign of France and Germany, 1944–1945* (Sidgwick and Jackson, 1981)

H. P. Willmott, *Empires in the Balance: Japanese and Allied Pacific Strategies, to April 1942* (Orbis, 1982)

C. Wilmot, *The Struggle for Europe* (Fontana, 1959)

Brigadier P. Young (ed), *The Almanac of World War II* (Bison/Hamlyn, 1981)

Brigadier P. Young (ed) and R. Natkiel (cartographer), *Atlas of the Second World War* (Weidenfeld and Nicolson, 1974).